HOW TO BECOME A
DATA SCIENTIST

A GUIDE FOR ESTABLISHED PROFESSIONALS

D1097521

By Adam Ross Nelson, JD PhD
Data Scientist

How to Become a Data Scientist: A Guide for Established Professionals
Nelson, Adam Ross, JD PhD

ISBN 979-8-9875037-0-6 hardcover
ISBN 979-8-9875037-1-3 paperback IS
ISBN 979-8-9875037-4-4 paperback
ISBN 979-8-9875037-2-0 eBook
ISBN 979-8-9875037-3-7 audiobook

Edited by Katie Beaton, Veneration Editorial.
Book production and cover design by Dawn James, Publish and Promote.
Interior layout and design by Perseus Design.
Cover art design by Adam Ross Nelson, JD PhD

Printed and bound in the United States of America.

Disclaimer:
The information contained in this book is for educational purposes. Any names, characters, businesses, places, events, or incidents are fictitious. Any resemblance to actual persons, living or dead, or actual events is purely coincidental. The views, thoughts, and opinions expressed in the text belong solely to the author, and not necessarily to the author's employer, organization, committee, or any other group or individual.

Expert Praises

Adam Ross Nelson leaves no stone unturned he provides readers with a roadmap to transition into the world of data science, by capitalizing on their current expertise. This book lays out step-by-step exactly how to break into data science as a mid to late-career professional. **- Jordan Goldmeier, Author of Becoming a Data Head.**

This book will save you years of time as you transition to becoming a Data Scientist. Data Science career coach expert Adam Ross Nelson demystifies the complex process of changing careers, quite literally walking readers through approachable steps on How to Become a Data Scientist. **- Kristina 'KP' Powers, Author of Second in Command, First in Excellence.**

Any experienced professional hoping to break into data needs this book because it strikes the right balance between strategic advice and pragmatic tips you can start applying today.

This book gives experienced professionals not just the tactical tips they need to break into a Data Science career, but something even more important – the confidence to make the leap! **– Nick Singh, Author of Ace the Data Science Interview & Founder of DataLemur.com**

Changing careers is challenging. From curating your resume, portfolio, and social media presence to interviewing and salary negotiation, coach Adam Ross Nelson guides you every step of the way to landing your first Data Scientist role. This book is filled with tips, resources, and advice that you will revisit throughout your new career. **- Stefanie Molin - Author of Hands-On Data Analysis with Pandas.**

A refreshing and inspiring look at how to transition to a career in data science along with practical advice and insights into the modern hiring process. I wish I had this guide when I made the switch from software engineering to data science! **- Frank La Vigne - Co-Host of the Data-Driven Podcast.**

Contents

Preface

An important reason I began writing this book was that I had noticed how other mid- and late-career professionals were seeking to make a similar transition as the one I had made in my late thirties. I went into data science after working primarily in higher education administration in my late twenties and early thirties.

This book reflects on the steps I took in making my career transition into data science. The truth though is that I made multiple career transitions. I went back and forth a bit between multiple paths, too. For example, as a teen, my first job ever was as a tour guide for a historic house museum. After high school but before college, I taught English as a second language in Budapest, Hungary. During college, I took some time away from classes to work for Mothers Against Drunk Driving as a school assembly speaker. After college, where I studied history and public communication, I worked in higher education administration. I continued teaching the occasional semester here and there. My career in higher education administration drove me to pursue a PhD in educational leadership and policy analysis. It was during the PhD program that I began to excel at statistics and data analytics.

A turning point for me was when I reached a spot in my career where I was working as a data scientist, but I was not formally in a data science role with my employer. I was doing the work of a data scientist. With an abundance of encouragement and support from friends, family, mentors, and co-workers, I transitioned formally into a data science role. I was the inaugural data scientist at the Common Application, Inc. In Chapter 2 of this book, I help you carefully dissect whether you too might be at a point in your career where you are already functionally a data scientist—if not yet formally one.

The advice in this book is the advice I would give to a close friend or a cherished family member—who is also a mid- or late-career professional. While much of the advice in this book may work well for professionals at any stage of their career, I worked to focus my advice for mid- and late-career professionals. If you have been frustrated in the past by the lack of advice specific to mid- and late-career professionals within the career advice genre, as I have been, this book aims to at least partially fill in this gap. For example, I thought deeply about what defines a mid- or late-career professional.

Within this book's advice, I comment on how or why this advice may specifically apply to mid- and late-career professionals. For another example, an overstated bit of advice in the career advice genre is to network, network, network. Yes, I do echo that advice in this book. However, I point out for readers how and why networking works differently for mid- and late-career professionals. I compassionately discuss how networking can bring a special source of anxiety and stress for mid- and late-career professionals. Younger professionals might not experience this anxiety in the same way. For a third example, to state the obvious, networking requires you to have a network. This is an asset that many mid- and late-career professionals already have as a natural function of their experience. Younger professionals have yet to acquire such a network.

I wrote this book by writing out the advice I was giving anyway. This advice is the advice I dispense as a career coach. I found myself giving the same advice over and over. I started writing some of this information online, mostly at https://medium.com.[1] Then, I created a handful of online courses. Eventually, I created personalized coaching programs designed for other data professionals looking to transition into data science.

It became apparent to me that much of the information available online or from other career service professionals did not speak to mid- or late-career professionals.

I hope you will find this book to be a useful resource as you consider making, and then proceeding with, your own professional career transition.

---

[1] Occasionally, I offer referral links, which may result in a commission I use to support the creation of new resources such as this book. For example, if you are not a member of Medium.com, consider joining via my referral link, which will provide you with access to the valuable news and information at Medium. A portion of your monthly subscription fee will also support my work: https://adamrossnelson.medium.com/membership

Introduction

Tell Us about Yourself

The first question you will get in any job interview will be something like, "Tell us about yourself."

As a mid- or late-career professional, you have likely faced this question many times. If you have been in a job interview (even just one interview), you have likely faced this question.

The key to preparing and delivering an impressive answer is knowing who you are. Likewise, the key to successfully transitioning your career is also knowing who you are (Nelson, 2022e).

I became a data scientist late in my career, after completing a PhD. I was around 38 years old. When anyone asks me to tell them about myself, my answer today is the same as it was when I went for my first data science interview many years ago.

I sat at a table across from four interviewers. I still remember the conference room. It was one of those rooms with heavy glass doors and large windows. Besides being in the middle of an interview, the use of glass in the environment made me feel like I was on display. I felt like the interviewers could see right through (me and the walls). After introductions, the first interviewer said, "Tell us a bit about yourself."

I felt my nerves relax because I had practiced. I knew who I was and why I was sitting at that table. I smiled and confidently told them, "I am extremely motivated by the opportunity to create new knowledge. I define new knowledge as information about how the world works that we have not previously possessed. Currently, my passion for new knowledge has pushed me toward my career in data science."

After my initial response, the second interviewer seemed to go off script. I think the second interviewer had a predetermined question to ask (based on the panel's intention to ask everyone the same set of questions). The second interviewer asked me to speak more about how I saw the connection between creating new knowledge, data science, and their organization's work.

I loved the question! It was exactly what I always hoped for in an interview—an opportunity for a genuine conversation and discussion. I explained, "For me, becoming a scientist, and more specifically a data scientist, allows me the opportunity to create and disseminate new knowledge on a full-time basis. If I worked for you, I would approach my work here as an opportunity to help you learn more about your data and about your operations based on that data."

Your Own Why

Finding and better understanding your own *why* is an important early step in making a major life transition…, such as moving from one career to another. When I work with others who aspire to enter or level up in data, I work to make sure they better understand who they are by finding or better exploring their own *why*.

Another reason to start the career transition process by thinking through this *tell us about yourself* question is because knowing your answer will help you to prepare and deliver an answer to the next question you will get 99% of the time: "Why are you interested in this job?"

You might think that you should give an answer specific to the job. When actually, the best answer will be about you. Your answer will connect who you are with your interest in the job.

The need to connect myself to the work hit home in another interview for the same position as I discussed above. I remember I was a bit nervous for this interview because on paper, I was not the most qualified. I wanted the position because it aligned with my *why*. The interviewer asked me, "Why are you interested in this position?" I paused because I knew this was my chance to showcase my interest in and enthusiasm for the data and topics I would work with in this specific position. This was my opportunity to bring home how well-suited I was to work in that specific position.

In template form, my response was:

I understand that you are looking for a data scientist who can work with [insert description of data specific to the job] *in order to better understand* [insert business problem specific to the employer]. *I am motivated by the opportunity to create new knowledge, and from an empirical perspective, the opportunities in this job to generate new knowledge are extensive. For that reason, I am thrilled to be a candidate interviewing for this position.*

The above works as a template because you can insert thoughts, ideas, and words specific to your situation within the places I gave square brackets.

Not Your First Rodeo

If you are reading this book, it is because you are a mid- or late-career professional. You have seen it all and then some. It is fair to say that you possess some combination of intelligence, ambition, resiliency, and other similar attributes. You have experienced and pushed through multiple struggles. The new world of data science likely is not your first rodeo—and it might not even be your last. I wrote this book for you.

The world of data science may seem overwhelmingly exciting. Simultaneously, as an experienced professional, when you look at it, you think, *This actually is not so new, is it?* You might think, *Has this not already been done before?* Or, *I have been around long enough to know that data science is a rebranding of techniques that advanced analysts have been using for decades.*

I am excited for you to get to know me and my path. I hope that doing so will help you on your own path. The middle and late portion of a person's career can be the most exciting portion of their career. You may think having major accomplishments is a young person's game. Perhaps you collected a few impressive accomplishments yourself at the beginning of your career. You can continue to have that flavor of success today, too. History shows us that many continue to achieve late into their careers.

Consider:

- Guido van Rossum was well into his thirties when he released the earliest versions of the Python programming language.
- Vera Wang had not designed her first dress until she was in her forties.
- Famed comic book author Stan Lee was nearly 40 when he first published *The Fantastic Four* in 1961.
- Toni Morrison published her first novel, *The Bluest Eye*, at the age of 39. She won her Pulitzer Prize for Fiction at the age of 57, and her Nobel Prize for Literature at the age of 62.
- Julia Child published her world-famous cookbook at the age of 49.

Google "anecdotes about success later in life" and read more if you are still not convinced. Just as this book's line edits were finishing up ChatGPT became available. I prompted ChatGPT to "Tell me some anecdotes about success late in life." Here are the results. *Colonel Sanders, the founder of Kentucky Fried Chicken, didn't begin franchising his famous chicken recipe until he was 65 years old. Before that, he had a variety of odd jobs, including running a service station and working as a tire salesman. Laura Ingalls Wilder, the author of the beloved "Little House on the Prairie" books, didn't publish her first book until she was 65 years old. Before that, she had been a homesteader, a schoolteacher, and a journalist.* You should try it too!

I want your next chapter in life (entering or leveling up in a data career) to be the best it can possibly be. If you want that too, keep reading.

Let me take you back to the year 2017. I was finishing my PhD studies and preparing for a career in academia. I was on my way, too. Honest to gosh. Here is how I got hired into my first data science role:

My supervisor at the time encouraged me to pursue data science. He spotted specific positions in which he thought I could succeed. He was confident in my ability to succeed as a data scientist, even though I had yet to work formally as a data scientist. I agreed with my supervisor that the position he had showed me was a good fit. The employer was asking for a data scientist who would work with precisely the data that I knew extremely well (from my current employment and from my PhD studies). Having recently completed a PhD, which relied on this flavor of data, I was arguably one of the world's few who knew this data extremely well.[2]

Despite knowing a lot about the data, I knew my skills and experiences did not fully match the position's description. There were some gaps. "I have not yet fully mastered the full range of desired experiences and knowledge as listed in the position description," I told my interviewer. Regardless of those gaps, the prospective employer invited me to interview on-site.

During that interview, I again noted that I had not yet fully mastered the full range of desired experiences and knowledge listed in the position's description. I have many vivid memories from the entire experience. Among those vivid memories are when the interviewer reminded me, "There is rarely, if ever, such a thing as a perfect candidate." The interviewer continued to say, "We anticipate needing to provide training and support to whomever we hire."

Throughout the interview, I became more interested in the role. I knew I could do a good job. I had a vision for how I could apply data science to their data. My parting words at the end of the interview expressed the following sentiment:

> *I looked at the original position description you sent around for this role, and I see that I am not the kind of candidate you had in mind. However, as I have had a chance to meet you through the*

---

[2] Note that PhD programs form graduates into the kinds of experts who know one specific thing (or a small set of things) really well. You know a lot about very little.

interview process, I think this role could be more than you had in mind, and I believe my background can help you make this role into that higher ideal. If your deliberations unfold in that way, I am eager to accept an offer from you for this job.

This is the story of a mid- or late-career professional seeking to transition into data science. This story involves myself as a candidate who was willing to speak with an employer about the advantages of hiring someone with a background that was unlike the background the employer initially sought. Having a unique or non-traditional background is a characteristic that many, if not all, mid- and late-career professionals have in common.

We have skills, abilities, experiences, and competencies that many other more junior (or traditional) candidates do not offer. Importantly, our skills, abilities, experiences, and competencies are qualities we bring as candidates that many employers do not seek (but can benefit them).

As mid- or late-career professionals, we should inventory these skills, abilities, experiences, and competencies. We have to inventory them so that we know them for ourselves (and this requires self-awareness). Then we must be able to communicate these skills, abilities, experiences, and competencies to employers. Successfully navigating that struggle to inventory my strengths and communicate them is a part of my story on how I transitioned into data science. Via this book, I will help you navigate that inventory and communication struggle. We can work on this together.

Tell Everyone about Yourself

Count the suggestion here in this introductory subsection as a quick win. Begin warming up your social media presence in anticipation of using social media as a component of a distributed professional portfolio strategy.

A step in the right direction is to post about your intentions as a user of social media. I suggest starting with LinkedIn, which is the main online venue for data science professionals seeking to interact with others they know, like, and trust.[3]

If you do not yet have a profile or an account on LinkedIn, it is free and easy to create. Later in this book, I offer detailed advice on how to update and configure your profile. Avoid worrying about being perfect right away. Start small.

Start by sharing about yourself. Decide for yourself how much you share, and when, and how. There are two ways to introduce and share something about yourself. You can do either, but I recommend doing both. First, you can update your biography section(s) on your social media profiles (LinkedIn calls it the "about" section). The second option, which is equally important, is to post a story about yourself. Make the story an interesting story about a lesson you learned, a book you read, or maybe a time you struggled but eventually triumphed.

Another step in the right direction would be to post about your intentions as a member of the platform. Write a post that identifies your area of expertise, your areas of interest, and

---

[3] See figure 6.1 in Chapter 6 of this book.

what your intentions are online. If you are looking for company, someone to join in, tag a colleague and challenge them to introduce themselves as well. Tag me if you would like, too!

This type of introductory post might read as follows:

I was recently reading a book that discussed the importance of stating your intentions as a member of a social media platform.

I decided to take this advice. Here on LinkedIn, you'll find me posting more and more in the near future. I hope to expand my professional network and find new relationships that can be mutually beneficial.

My interests are data science, machine learning, artificial intelligence, statistics, and advanced analytics (or data in general). Connect with me or give me a follow if you have similar interests.

Perhaps we'll be able to share information with each other that will help each other out. And I wouldn't rule out the opportunity to help each other with our careers down the road.

Adam Ross Nelson, 🔲 **Data Science Career S...** (He/Him) • You • • •
Ask about data science career services @ Coaching.AdamRossNelson.c...

Happy Memorial Day Weekend (US) folks. Happy weekend to all.

I was recently writing out some advice that discussed the importance of stating your intentions as a member of a social media platform.

I decided to take this advice. Here on LinkedIn you'll find me posting more and more in the near future.

I hope to expand my professional network and find new relationships that can be mutually beneficial.

My interests are data science, machine learning, artificial intelligence, statistics, and advanced analytics (or data in general). Connect with me or give me a follow if you have similar interests.

Perhaps we'll be able to share information with each other that will help each other out. And I wouldn't rule out the opportunity to help each other with our careers down the road.

#datascience #machinelearning #artificialintelligence #statistics

These example posts (written out and pictured above) explain to others how connecting with you or following you will enrich their experience on the platform. If and when folks connect with you, accept the connection requests. Then follow through. Speak with your new connections; make conversation. For everyone who connects with you (and whom you decide to connect with too), send that new connection a note. Start conversations.

If that new connection writes you a note, be sure to respond to their note. And whether or not that new connection sends you a note, make sure you browse their profile. Find a point of interest or a common attribute or experience you both share. In your message, give a comment or a remark (and a reflection) on that shared attribute or experience.

An effort to start that new relationship with a small conversation will do two things. It will help personalize your experience and the experience of others. It will also preserve a record of what drew you to each other. Later, sometimes years later, I have found my message history to be a valuable record of how and why I connected with others online.

For folks who are starting out on LinkedIn, aim to achieve these three goals in all of your communications online:

1. authenticity
2. openness
3. helpfulness

These three attributes will show others that connecting with you is mutually beneficial.

Standard, Incidental, and Strategic Transitions

Before moving into the rest of this book, I encourage readers to think systematically about the process of transitioning into data science. A hallmark of a data scientist's work is that we approach problems in exceedingly systematic ways. To begin thinking systematically about your transition, consider the kind of transition you are contemplating.

I have broken career transitions into three kinds of transitions, including the standard, the incidental, and the strategic.

Standard Transitions

Standard career transitions represent a progressive growth with an employer (e.g., from assistant to associate). Sometimes, standard career transitions include a modest change in responsibility and salary. These transitions often mean keeping existing supervisory relationships and may be accompanied by moderate increases in pay or other benefits. These transitions usually involve remaining with the same employer before, during, and following the transition.

The purpose of these transitions is for the sake of advancement. From the employer's perspective, they can improve retention by giving employees a sense of career progression through a predetermined ladder. This means that standard career transitions are often highly predictable and a part of the organization's "standard" career ladder progression. These transitions may or may not recognize the employee for the full extent of their value, which would include the employee's new skills and abilities acquired while employed by the employer. The standard career transition may technically represent a promotion, but the accompanying raise in pay or boost in title could fall short of fully recognizing the employee's value.

Incidental Transitions

Incidental transitions represent a change in employment due to factors that are not related to career advancement. This means that the career transition is incidental to other life or industry changes. Examples of incidental career transitions are: personnel reductions, layoffs, company closure, and other forces above and beyond the employer's or employee's scope of control.

Incidental career transitions may require relocation due to one's spouse's career transition (e.g. moving across the country for a new job). Many professionals make incidental career transitions for other personal reasons, such as the need to care for parents, family, or newborn children.

Strategic Transitions

A strategic transition often means a change in field. Frequently a change for which the employee planned or aspired. Strategic career transitions can be vertical. A vertical transition would sometimes involve significant advances in compensation and levels of professional responsibility. Strategic career transitions may also involve lateral moves from one functional area to another. For example, someone might move from accounting to data science or from marketing to event management. Lateral strategic career transitions are also beneficial for professionals who seek to transition from one industry to another.

If you are experiencing or anticipating a standard or an incidental career transition, as you move through this book, consider how its advice can help you convert that transition into a strategic transition.

Conclusion

The very first step on your journey to transition into a data science career is one of self-reflection. Think deeply about your *why*. What are the real reasons behind your desire to work as a data scientist? Your *why* will lead to the answers to two commonly asked interview questions: *tell us about yourself* and *why are you interested in this job?*

I have shared my own experiences as I transitioned into data science. My story highlights how, from the employer's perspective, there is almost never a perfect candidate. The notion that a perfect candidate does not exist means that you have more opportunity than you might think. Because I was honest and persistent, and with support from others, I eventually transitioned into data science. This book is a collection of the advice I formulated for myself and others along my own journey.

In the latter part of this introduction, I encouraged you to consider what kind of career transition you are seeking. Thinking systematically about whether your transition is standard, incidental, or strategic will help you understand your motivations better. If you are facing a standard or incidental transition, consider ways to convert that transition into something more strategic.

This book aims to help mid- and late-career professionals transition into data science. There is a tremendous potential for achievement later on in one's career. Many mid- and late-career professionals have unique employment histories that may not exactly align with a new career in data science. Do not let this apparent misalignment deter you from exploring. This book will help you in explaining how your unique background can be to your new employer's advantage.

This introduction included ideas to warm up your professional social media accounts in preparation for using them to aid in your career transition. My key advice for social media is to be authentic, open, and helpful.

CHAPTER 1

Who Is a Mid- or Late-Career Professional?

There are two ways to think about this question. The first way takes a categorical approach. The second way takes a more qualitative and inclusive approach, which better accounts for potential edge cases. After discussing both the categorical and the inclusive approach, this chapter will review the skills, abilities, experiences, and professional assets that mid- and late-career professionals have worked very hard to gain and build over the course of their careers. To prepare for interviews, candidates should use this chapter as a reminder of how to communicate the value mid- and late-career professionals offer employers.

The Categorical Approach

When working to define mid- and late-career professionals, the categorical approach is to list out a set of criteria that defines the term *mid- or late-career professional*. Here are criteria to which I often point:

PhD/EdD Holders

The U.S. Census Bureau estimates that 13.1% of adults have a master's, professional degree, or doctorate. From 2000 to 2018, the number of individuals in this category doubled (America Counts Staff, 2019). Those with a doctorate have executed an original research project and completed the dissertation defense process. They fit into this book's definition of a mid- and late-career professional because, through the dissertation proposal and defense process, they have demonstrated their *ability to lead and execute large and complex multi-year projects*. Two of the hallmark characteristics of mid- and late-career professionals are time served in full-time professional roles and a proven ability to lead and execute large and complex projects. Completing the PhD and dissertation process requires time and shows that ability to execute large and complex projects.

Master's Degree Holders (+ 4 to 6 Years as a Full-time Professional)

Those who have completed a master's while having worked four to six years or more also fit into the category of mid- or late-career professionals. For many, having completed a master's degree alone shows prowess on matters related to independently leading and executing large and complex projects, which is necessary to qualify as a mid- or late-career professional. As an additional guide, I often look to see 4 to 6 years of full-time professional work as part of these criteria. The 4 to 6 years of full-time work combined with the master's degree is what sets apart these professionals, as they also have the solid skills, abilities, and experiences that provide the value associated with being a mid- or late-career professional.

Those with 6 to 12 Years of Full-time Professional Experience in at Least One Industry

Hard work and persistent dedication over nearly or more than a decade is a path that will earn a professional the skills, abilities, and experiences that provide the value associated with being a mid- or late-career professional.

***

I point to the categorical criteria above with some measure of reluctance. The categorical approach makes it appear that transitioning into data science is an exclusive opportunity that is open to only a privileged few. The opposite is the case.

Before moving to the second definition of mid- and late-career professionals, notice there is not necessarily a minimum level of education. The criteria are broad and flexible. For this book, the definition of a mid- or late-career professional is intentionally broad. This book seeks to open gates and remove barriers—not to reinforce them.

Mid- or Late-Career Edge Cases

The second definition of a mid- or late-career professional I offer here is much more inclusive. If, after reviewing the categorical approach above, you are still not sure whether you are a mid- or late-career professional, you may be an edge or corner case. This section offers a measure of the special handling you may need, and certainly also deserve.

The opportunity to transition into data science as a mid- or late-career professional is much more open than the above categorical criteria may suggest. I offer this second qualitative and inclusive approach to defining mid- and late-career professionals to avoid the false impression that data science is a profession that only belongs to elite, highly educated professionals (or only to those professionals who are educated and who pursued their career in a hyper-specific way).

This second, more qualitative and inclusive approach could be thought of as a collection of edge or corner cases.

Some examples:

➤ Professionals who have completed one or more bootcamps designed to teach coding, software engineering, data science, or other specific technical skills.

➤ Professionals who started, but did not yet finish, an advanced degree.

➤ Professionals who have no undergraduate degree but who have many years (or decades) of experience.[4]

➤ Professionals who have not yet acquired 6 to 12 years of *full-time* professional experience but who have worked *part time*.[5]

 ○ For example, some professionals may have stayed home for significant portions of their adult life to care for the home and family.

➤ Professionals who experienced extended absences from the workforce for personal health reasons.[6]

---

[4] 19.3% of the United States population above the age of 25 have completed some college but not a degree (American Community Survey, 2021); According to the Chronical of Higher Education, adult populations in all states with some college but no degree ranged from 12.6% to 26.1% (2022).

[5] This group may include between 63,288,000 and 97,866,000 employed adults in the United States (U.S. Bureau of Labor Statistics, 2022b).

[6] The number of professionals who experienced extended absences is not well measured. However, the U.S. Bureau of Labor Statistics estimates that in one month alone (January of 2022), 7.8 million workers had an illness-related work absence (U.S. Bureau of Labor Statistics, 2022a).

Edge Cases Are Common

According to Wikipedia (2022c), an edge case "typically involves input values that require special handling." A related idea in software, data science, and engineering is *corner case*. According to Wikipedia (2022b), corner cases include "situation[s] that occurs only outside normal operating parameters."

By analogy, you might be a candidate who is an edge or corner case. In the world of employment, edge and corner case candidates are common. I included extensive references to employment and population statistics in this section to remind edge case candidates that they are not alone. In fact, they are likely in good company.

The qualitative and inclusive approach to identifying mid- and late-career professionals shows how the door is open for edge and corner cases, too. This book's purpose is to break down barriers and open doors. Recruiters and hiring managers are the gatekeepers to this rewarding profession. This book is not the gatekeeper. I designed this book to help you work with gatekeepers so that they will see the brilliance and value you bring to the profession.

Categorical criteria often miss the point. The second approach to defining a mid- and late-career data professional looks more toward an important point: Mid- and late-career professionals bring skills, abilities, capabilities, and experiences with them that younger professionals often do not.

A crucial aspect that mid- and late-career professionals need to understand for themselves, and also know how to communicate, is that employers have difficulty finding the skills, abilities, capabilities, and experiences that mid-and late-career professionals possess. When hiring professionals who are early in their career, it is challenging to find the skills and abilities that mid- and late-career professionals already have spent their careers acquiring.

The Assets of a Mid- or Late-Career Professional

This book helps mid- and late-career professionals find clarity on the skills, abilities, capabilities, and experiences they bring to the workplace. Each reader will have a unique set of skills, abilities, capabilities, and experiences. Take inventory of what you are good at (and where you might need help).

What follows is an overview of various skill sets and how mid- and late-career professionals acquired them.

Administrative Experience

This type of experience involves rudimentary tasks and skills. Many mid- and late-career professionals have long mastered administrative tasks. An employer who hires a mid- or late-career professional will not need to teach that employee about how to file documents, distribute documents through an organization, take meeting notes, or manage multiple schedules.

The soft skills associated with administrative experience are:

- A knowledge of filing systems.
- The ability to preserve a record (and understanding the importance of preserving a record).
- Multitasking.
- Seeing opportunities to contribute to the team (and doing so).
- Time management.

Management Experience

There are at least two flavors of management. Many mid- or late-career professionals will bring skills and experiences with both flavors. There is management of people, and there is management of "things" (i.e., projects or resources). Building either flavor of management experience requires years of work. Mid- and late-career professionals must learn to identify their management experience and sell it as an asset when communicating with prospective recruiters, hiring managers, and co-workers.

For example, mid- and late-career professionals should be able to speak fluently about their experience in budgeting, accounting, and bookkeeping. Also important, as a manager, are the abilities to allocate resources—often in the face of competing priorities. Related experience might involve interviewing others and then selecting from a pool of candidates in the process of building a team. Management experience common for mid- and late-career professionals involves managing change for themselves and their team or project.

Supervisory Experience

A supervisor is a person who is responsible for the work of other professionals. At some organizations, the terms *supervisor* and *manager* may be synonymous.

Many mid- and late-career professionals bring with them skills specifically related to supervising other people, including preparing and delivering constructive feedback of others. An important part of this area of experience is the ability to evaluate the performance of others. Mid- and late-career professionals with supervisory experience will know how to manage interpersonal conflict and resolve work-related disputes. Supervisors bring skills and experiences related to scheduling that is above and beyond administrative scheduling and calendar management. Mid- and late-career professionals know how to help others manage tasks and work successfully. In these ways, mid- and late-career professionals are good at contributing to the success of others.

Strategic Experience

Strategic experience is a type of experience mid- and late-career professionals need to showcase. Professionals acquire this type of experience by regularly thinking about the purpose of their work, the purpose of the team's work, the purpose of the organization's work, and how these purposes align (or misalign). Strong strategic thinkers, as many mid- and late-career professionals may be, know how to identify misalignments and then use the savviest mix of resources in correcting those misalignments.

Mid- and late-career professionals can improve their ability to show their skills and abilities related to strategy by emphasizing how their mindset focuses on the organization's main purposes, efficiencies, inefficiencies, customer experiences, employee experiences, and the financial bottom line.

Leadership Experience

Successful mid- and late-career professionals usually offer piles of leadership experience. A strong leader both encourages and inspires others around them. Mid- and late-career professionals with leadership experience can facilitate an atmosphere in which people are happy and motivated. The leadership that mid- and late-career professionals offer can also involve helping other employees feel valued, heard, and respected. Even more importantly, mid- and late-career professionals who have leadership experience know how to keep others on task. These leadership experiences include demonstrated skills and abilities in listening, keeping an open mind, recognizing bias, and asking critical questions.

For example, a mid- or late-career professional understands that the decision-making process may sometimes need to move quickly, but that at other times, it may need to move with greater deliberation. A mid- or late-career professional who leads well can bring the measured and steady source of wisdom that comes from that open-minded way of thinking.

Leadership experience grows over time. One of the many reasons mid- and late-career professionals bring strong leadership experience with them is that they have acquired and demonstrated their leadership skills both at work and in the community. Mid- and late-career professionals with extensive community connections often apply and grow their leadership skills in social, civic, and professional organizations. When mid- and late-career professionals speak about their leadership experiences (during an interview, for example), it is important to give extensive mention to their leadership experience outside of the workplace.

Professional Network

This category of skills, abilities, and experiences is more extrinsic than many of the other categories discussed above. A professional network refers to the business and personal contacts gained from years of working. These contacts include past and present colleagues, fellow members of professional associations, former mentors or professors, and current and former mentees. They are a reliable group for assistance, information, and business opportunities.

It takes years to develop a professional network. Some mid- and late-career professionals may be better at building, nurturing, and maintaining a professional network than others of course, but as discussed above, all mid- and late-career professionals have benefited from the support, advice, and guidance of others. Mid- and late-career professionals who transition from one career to another bring to their new career the same support, advice, and guidance that had helped them succeed in their earlier career.

When showcased well, this personal network is an asset that is attractive to prospective employers. The reason this can, or should be, attractive to prospective employers is that a professional network acts as a source of assistance, information, and business development for the employer's benefit, too.

Credibility

Professional credibility is a source of legitimacy. We build it over years of professional experience by showing our capability to execute responsibilities properly, accomplish goals, and deliver on expectations.

Individuals steadily gain professional credibility by consistently being trustworthy, competent, genuine, respectful, and accountable. This deep well of credibility is one reason companies that prioritize credibility often hire mid- and late-career professionals, as they are highly capable, well-known, widely liked, and trusted.

Chapter Summary

After reading this chapter, you may find that you are in fact a mid- or late-career professional, whether by the more exclusive parameters of the categorical approach or within the more inclusive edge and corner case criteria I presented. And you may be feeling uncertain about a career transition into data science.

Consider this: There rarely, if ever, is such a thing as a candidate who is perfect for a position. Let us be real. Nobody is perfect. However, being a mid- or late-career professional means you already have applicable skills that are in demand.

These skills may include the following skill sets:

- administrative
- management
- supervisory
- strategic
- leadership

An added point to note is that you possess a professional network that is likely more extensive than those who are in an earlier stage of their career. That network, which is the result of your credibility, can be as much for your prospective employer's benefit as it can be for your own benefit.

My goal for this chapter is to empower you to transition into data science with confidence. That confidence will come from fully understanding your strengths and the professional assets you offer.

The full process of transitioning into data science from start to finish is more than I can present in one chapter. The rest of this book outlines additional must-know strategies and considerations I learned from personal experience as I made the transition.

CHAPTER 2

What Is Data Science?

After defining what data science is and providing an inspirational look at the often-untold history of data science, this chapter will look at the future of data science. In looking at that future, this chapter will offer insight into the professional outlook for those who work in data science. Lastly, this chapter will introduce three characters whom I will reference throughout this book. Their names are Daveed (ze, zim, zis), Poleh (she, her, hers), and Jodi (they, them, theirs).

Data science is an interdisciplinary area of practice and research involving scientific processes, advanced mathematics, computer programming, statistics, data mining, text processing, and other related notions. One of the main problems facing data science practitioners is that it is difficult to find individual professionals who possess both the right mix of data science skills and the right mix of practical experience outside of data science. This practical experience outside of data science is what data scientists call *domain knowledge.*

Domain Knowledge

Domain knowledge is a specialty form of knowledge. This specialty knowledge often has very little to do with the core components of data science work. Domain knowledge is knowledge that you learn on the job, through years of work in any field. Professionals gain this specialty knowledge through advanced academic study, special corporate training, or sheer force of on-the-job experience. Domain knowledge could be knowledge of the retail industry, for example. Another type of domain knowledge could be knowledge related to health care, medicine, or pharmaceuticals. Other specific areas of domain knowledge are accounting, human resources, marketing, manufacturing, construction, and city management (Nelson, 2022c).

For example, later in this chapter, I will introduce you to three fictional characters who also transitioned into data science. You will meet Daveed, who worked in education earlier in his career. As a result of zis experience in education, ze could present zimself as a data scientist with domain knowledge related to student, teacher, and school data. You will then meet Poleh, who worked in marketing and in firms that managed electronic medical records. To give her a boost in her transition into data science, she leveraged her knowledge of the business processes specific to marketing electronic medical record services. A third character, Jodi, leveraged domain knowledge of pharmaceutical data as they transitioned into data science.

The most important aspect of domain knowledge is that for those who possess a deep understanding of specific domains, they will also understand the business problems of those domains. Understanding a business problem is not something that otherwise comes naturally for data scientists fresh out of college or still early on in their careers. Thus, for the mid- or late-career professional, data science is an opportunity for career advancement by combining advanced domain knowledge with data science.

Skills Gap

The future of data science is bright. According to the U.S. Bureau of Labor Statistics Occupational Outlook Handbook (OOH), computer and information research scientists (one of the handbook's best euphemisms for data science) earn a median annual income of $131,490 per year. In other words, data scientists potentially earn almost three times the median annual income of "all occupations" (OOH, 2022). The OOH listed the anticipated 2021–2031 growth rate for the field at 21%, compared to the growth rate for all occupations at 5%.

Now is a great time to be or become a data scientist! And yet, one of the fundamental problems facing this industry is what many call *the skills gap.* The first side of the skills gap is experience. Contemporary notions of data science remain new enough that the market of available data scientists does not yet have a ton of data scientists with "data science" degrees. What the market does have are smart, quantitatively minded, and inquisitive folks who can be data scientists once they know how to communicate their skills correctly. (That is you.)

Another gap in the industry is a gap between those with the technical understanding and know-how in data science and those with deep and meaningful domain knowledge. While a few junior employees have bona fide data science degrees or certificates from powerful, brand-name bootcamps (a competitive advantage for sure), only mid- or late-career professionals (like you) possess this deep domain knowledge.

If you doubt whether data science is right for you, by the end of this chapter, you will have a better understanding of what data science is, where it came from, where it is going, and how you can fit into the world of data science.

The Inspirational History of Data Science

The first ever data scientist in the world might surprise you. If you are like me, the story of the first ever data scientist may also inspire you.

Some might point to Peter Naur or John Tukey. Sure, these two are prominent figures, but Peter Naur was not the first data scientist, and neither was John Tukey.

Many credit Peter Naur with having originated the term *data science* around 1974. Naur also used the term *dataology* (Wikipedia, 2022d). Others point to John Tukey, who published an article on the future of data analysis in a 1962 edition of *The Annals of Mathematical Statistics*. Tukey's contribution to notions that eventually became known as "data science" began when he questioned the adequacy of the term *data analysis*. Without specifically coining the term *data science*, Tukey coined a definition that approached the modern definition. Tukey wrote a definition that might approach many definitions of data science or other synonymous terms, such as *advanced business analytics*: "Some parts of data analysis . . . are allocation, in the sense that they guide us in the distribution of effort and other valuable considerations in observation, experimentation, or analysis. Data analysis is a larger and more varied field than inference" (Tukey 1962, 2).

A deeper analysis brings us back nearly 150 years before Naur and Tukey. Ada Lovelace[7] contributed to science, mathematics, computing, and data analysis. Lovelace recognized that computers (not yet then called computers) could be useful beyond simple calculations. People widely recognize her as the person who published the first formal algorithm and thus consider her to be the first computer programmer or computer scientist (Wikipedia, 2022a).

In her notes, she wrote, *like a data scientist*, saying:

---

[7] Augusta Ada King, Countess of Lovelace (née Byron). December 10, 1815 – November 27, 1852.

Supposing, for instance, that the fundamental relations of pitched sounds in the science of harmony and of musical composition were susceptible of such expression and adaptations, the engine might compose elaborate and scientific pieces of music of any degree of complexity or extent (Hooper, 2012).

I am a fan of Ada's story because her experience exemplifies one of this book's most important lessons: Nobody needs to call you a data scientist for you to do data science work. Like Lovelace, you might already be a data scientist, but you just do not know it yet. You do not need to be "trained as a data scientist" (whatever that might mean) to be called or hired as a data scientist. Data scientists come from many backgrounds.

Data scientists' backgrounds are sufficiently varied, so much so that it almost seems that data scientists often come from no background, much in the same way Lovelace became a data scientist or a computer programmer with no formal training in data science or computer science. At least not in the terms that we would consider formal for many of today's career preparation purposes. At the time, data science and computer science did not exist yet, not formally. Every professional has to come from some place. Every professional has to start some place.

The purpose of data science evolved into a study or practice of finding meaningful information in raw facts, figures, and data. As the abundance of data proliferated, the demand for making meaning of that data also grew. The daily rate of data generation as of the first edition of this book numbered in the quintillions of bytes (Vuleta, 2021). To give you some perspective on that number: A quintillion is a number that includes 18 decimal places left of the decimal point. One quintillion is a million trillion (1,000,000 x 1,000,000,000,000).

Aided by the growth in the volume of data since the inception of data science (whenever you date its inception), many industries have benefited from the field's insights. Today, whether most consumers know or realize it, data science touches every aspect of business, social, cultural, civic, and governmental life.

Traits of a Data Scientist

Data scientists are inquisitive and critical thinkers from many backgrounds. Another way to define data science, and know if it might be right for your career transition, is to examine the common traits of a data scientist.

Note that these traits are not a list of requirements. No two data scientists are alike. And reasonable people may disagree on this list of traits. Use this list of traits as a general guide to understand the field and how you might enjoy working in the field.

A Curious Mind

If you are curious about how the world works, then you may have the curiosity that is characteristic of many data scientists.

If you have a curious mind, data science may be the perfect field for you.

Curious minds do not usually allow questions to intimidate them. Asking and tackling tough questions will lead to experimentation, which will lead to results. A curious mind understands that it does not matter if an experiment produces the expected results. Each experiment reveals new insight and information, and this is what fuels a curious mind. When data scientists cannot find an answer to a question, they will continue to ask questions until they find an answer that satisfies their curiosity.

If you have experienced the instinct to keep investigating, even beyond the point where many others may have discontinued their effort, then considering data science is a smart choice for you.

An Instinct for Finding, Recognizing, and Explaining Patterns

One of the most crucial skills a data scientist can have is the ability to extract information from not-so-obvious facts and figures. In data science, we often rely heavily on our knowledge of computer algorithms to extract that information. What makes for especially effective data scientists are the instincts associated with finding and extracting that information. As advanced and sophisticated as the algorithms are, selecting and applying the best choice of algorithms requires human instinct and intuition. This brand of instinct involves bringing multiple perspectives to our analytical work.

As data scientists, we must work with multiple perspectives and hypotheses. This means that professionals with a background in qualitative research (e.g. academic researchers, user experience researchers, focus group researchers, or interview researchers) are strong candidates for data science.

Ability to Learn New Analytical Techniques

The range of techniques available to data science and the range of the most popular techniques are constantly changing. Mid- and late-career professionals not only need an ability and willingness to learn new analytical techniques at the beginning of their career transition but also going forward, as each project will require a unique mix of techniques.

To be a data scientist means you are constantly learning. As technology is changing and updating at a rapid speed, the ability to adapt to new trends is a must. Old technologies wash out quickly, while new technologies survive the day. To be competitive as a data scientist (and to position yourself as someone who can solve more than one kind of analytical problem), you need to understand how to triage problems. You then need to understand how to find, and then learn, new analytical techniques that are specifically applicable to each new problem when it arrives on your desk.

Patience When Things Do Not Work at First

Data science deals with big data, and the results are not instantaneous. Sometimes, the results do not even make sense at first. Patience and consistency are necessary traits and skills that a data scientist must have. When I provide training for managers and executives who oversee teams that produce data science products and services, one of my key messages is to consider how much time a properly planned and managed data science project requires. I teach that it is crucial for managers and executives to allocate sufficient time for the entire process. Figure 2.1 shows a customary data science process. To read Figure 2.1, start at the upper left with *Question or Problem* and then move clockwise around the diagram.

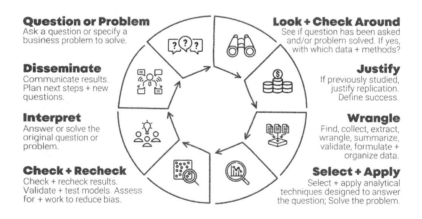

Question or Problem
Ask a question or specify a
business problem to solve.

Look + Check Around
See if question has been asked
and/or problem solved. If yes,
with which data + methods?

Disseminate
Communicate results.
Plan next steps + new
questions.

Justify
If previously studied,
justify replication.
Define success.

Interpret
Answer or solve the
original question or
problem.

Wrangle
Find, collect, extract,
wrangle, summarize,
validate, formulate +
organize data.

Check + Recheck
Check + recheck results.
Validate + test models. Assess
for + work to reduce bias.

Select + Apply
Select + apply analytical
techniques designed to answer
the question; Solve the problem.

Figure 2.1

There is a need for patience whenever any of these eight steps in the data science process require more time than expected. Another reason patience matters is because the process is actually not cyclical, even though this diagram presents it that way. A project might reach a later stage but then need to return to an earlier stage for additional preparatory work.

Unanticipated surprises can occur at any stage in this process. An example of an unanticipated surprise is encountering documentation related to a crucial tool on which the project relies but that the team overlooked earlier. Another common surprise is when the team finds records or publications that previously answered the question or solved the problem but that the team missed during the *Look and Check Around* step.

For yet another example, a project may reach the *Interpret* stage before the team realizes one or more oversights occurred earlier during the *Wrangle* stage. Finding such an oversight will require the team to step backward, to correct the oversight, and then move again back forward through the process.

These surprises mean projects will need to briefly revisit earlier steps. Thus, the process is more iterative than this cyclical diagram implies and involves researching how others have approached similar projects. The non-linear and iterative nature of data science work requires patience.

An Interest in and a Familiarity with Process Design or Development

The reason process design and development matters is that our work in data science is often best executed when there is a process in place to guide our work. This chapter's discussion of data science processes also serves to help candidates speak at interviews and through other conversations during the job search process. There are at least as many data science processes as there are data science teams. Each book, training program, or expert seems to present this process using different terms.

For examples, see the following articles from my reference list in the back of this book: Kirill's "The Data Science Process," Palachy's "Data Science Project Flow for Startups," and Nantasenamat's "The Data Science Process." When reviewing a process, note that no single process can be more correct than another. The key take-away from previously documented processes is that data science teams need both to discuss and to decide what their process will be and then document that process for their own use and purposes.

When I am teaching about the data science process, I emphasize two things:

1. There is no right or wrong way to articulate the process.
2. The most important part of the process is merely having a process.

Organizations and teams who have not yet documented their analytical or data science processes can upgrade their data savviness and literacy by having a conversation that seeks to explore and document the process.

For readers who have yet to think through what the data science process can or should look like for themselves or their teams, the following briefly elaborates on each of the stages listed in Figure 2.1.

For this chapter, I will call the first stage *Question or Problem*. Please do not let the shorthand obscure the dynamic nature associated with this first stage. It might sound more like specifying research questions in terms related to a specific business problem or objective. For a bookseller, for example, the business objective or research question might be "How can we anticipate what books each customer will be most interested in purchasing?"

I typically call the second stage *Look and Check Around*. This second stage is merely background research to see if anyone has asked and answered the question. Organizations that are highly data-driven will have an organized and easily searchable record of previous research questions that the organization studied. Searching publicly available sources of research findings is important as well. During the *Look and Check Around* stage, you will discover which similar questions have been studied or which similar business problems have been solved. For future reference later in the project, this stage also involves identifying what data sources previous efforts referenced and what methods previous efforts applied.

When there has been extensive study of the research question, or if the business problem is already well understood (and solved), the team needs to decide if there is sufficient justification to replicate the work. This justification happens in the step labeled *Justify* in Figure 2.1. During the justification, it is useful to define success or ascertain how you will measure the project's return on investment.

Following justification comes the *Wrangle* step. Assuming the research will progress after the *Justify* stage, the team will then proceed to the fourth stage. This data wrangling step involves obtaining the data that will be necessary for future steps ahead. Finding the data means determining if the data already exists, and if so, what would be involved in extracting the data. Finding the data might mean collecting new data.

After finding the data, the *Wrangle* stage then involves cleaning and preparing the data. An example of cleaning or preparing data is checking to make sure the data "makes sense." Consider a data set that includes date of birth and date of death. Imagine that the data are from records of hospital residents in the late 1800s. A data cleaning procedure could involve checking to make sure the dates of deaths are all after the dates of birth. Related, one would need to check that the dates are all before 1900. If any of the dates of death were somehow listed as occurring before dates of birth, the data wrangling, cleaning, preparing, and validation procedures would involve deciding what to do with the apparently erroneous records.

The *Wrangle* stage will often include summarizing the data. The team will need to look back on how the data were prepared, so a robust round of descriptive statistics and visualizations will be helpful during later stages.

All stages entail input from data scientists, but the fifth stage (*Select and Apply*) and the sixth stage (*Check and Recheck*) are the stages in which data scientists shine brightest. Alternatively, I refer to the fifth step as *modeling* and the sixth step as *validating*. During this fifth stage, the primary tasks are selecting and then applying one or more analytical techniques. In the bookstore example, the team might look to apply random forests to anticipate in which genre the customer will be most interested.

After modeling with random forests, the team would then progress to *validating*, the sixth stage, where the team checks and rechecks the results. During this stage, the team will accomplish multiple tasks. It is important to validate the results on new data and to test the model. Testing the model can involve using hold-out or set-aside data—or it can involve testing the model in production. During this sixth stage is when teams will assess their work for bias and other weaknesses. Where teams find bias, they should work to reduce that bias, perhaps by revisiting the work completed in earlier stages. Where teams find limitations, it will be necessary to document those limitations or work to mitigate them.

In the last two stages, *Interpret* and then *Disseminate*, it is critical to fully interpret the results in terms (words, phrases, and visuals) that non-data scientists can read and understand. The goal is to answer the analytical question or to specify a solution to the business problem. Dissemination is about communication. This last stage can involve preparing a hand-off for product engineers and others throughout the larger organization, who will put the solution into production.

Putting the bookseller hypothetical into production would mean creating a way for the seller's website to calculate in which genre a customer will be most interested based on the random forest model. Then a model-enhanced website can provide customers with offers specific to that genre. Another production example could be a system that decides what topics to discuss when the bookseller sends e-mails or postal mail to that customer.

My favorite part of the last stage, *Disseminate*, is planning for next steps. Planning ahead means looking over the previous stages plus the results and identifying new research questions or business problems, which the team can then iteratively put back into the process by starting over on the first step, *Question or Problem*.

A Love for Finding, Cleaning, and Organizing Data

I am unreasonably obsessed with the statistic that data scientists report spending 80% of their time finding, cleaning, and organizing data. This statistic is according to a modest sample of data scientists analyzed by the Harvard Business Review (Bowne-Anderson, 2018). It is our job to make sense of data and then generate new knowledge. Before finding those meaningful patterns and proceeding to generate new knowledge, we have to prepare that data. The data we work with is often messy and unorganized. This data can come from many sources, including surveys, experiments, social media, and transaction data. Once we have found relevant data, we must then clean it. This cleaning process includes identifying and removing errors, outliers, and missing values. For me, finding, cleaning, and organizing data is part of the thrill. If you find similar pleasure in these tasks, you also demonstrate a key characteristic common to many data scientists. Finding, cleaning, and organizing data can be a challenging yet rewarding process.

A Love for Technology

If you are the type of person who likes to tinker and find new ways to do things, data science is definitely a field for you to consider. If technology amazes you, and you can think strategically and analytically about the benefits and drawbacks of technology, then data science is for you. You may also have a history of learning new technologies and finding novel ways to apply them.

Not only should you firmly ingrain a love for technology into how you think about life and work, but you should be known for it. As a mid- or late-career professional, perhaps you were among the first to suggest that your employer adopt a range of technologies that are now well-accepted but were new only 10, 15, or maybe 20 years ago.

One of the many reasons data science is a good career choice for those who deeply appreciate technology is that being a data scientist can be about devising new technologies. For example, besides developing innovative ways to analyze data, you may also play an important role in devising new ways to store, distribute, share, secure, and otherwise manage data. A data scientist who is a technologist can have a significant impact not only on the field of data science but also on the world at large.

A Love and Acumen for Communication

There is a story in my career that I am somewhat shy to tell. I had been a data scientist for some time when a co-worker asked me a stunningly difficult-to-hear question at work. It was a question that made me realize I had made a huge mistake (Nelson, 2020b).

The question was: "When do you think we will start using machine learning, artificial intelligence, and predictive modeling?" The problem was that we had already been using data science. Apparently, we had not yet communicated that usage so well.

Many organizations have used data science and related analytical techniques for a long time. As an established professional, the understanding or intuition that data science is a rebranding of earlier practices in advanced analytics may be familiar to you. As with many aspects of succeeding in business, a successful data science practice consists of sheer high-quality communication. After all, data scientists are often working with people who are not data scientists. We need to explain our work clearly and concisely. Achieving this communication can be a challenge, but it is one that data scientists need to meet. The added measure of communications experience mid- and late-career professionals bring with them as data science candidates is another reason we are well-suited for the field. If you enjoy this kind of challenge and feel you are skilled in meeting this kind of challenge, data science is a career option for you to consider.

The Future of Data Science

Data worldwide (stored, copied, etc.) by 2025 may reach somewhere near 175 (Vuleta, 2021) to 181 (Statista, n.d.) zettabytes. A zettabyte is a thousand exabytes. One exabyte is one thousand petabytes. One petabyte is a thousand terabytes. And a terabyte is a thousand megabytes. This is a lot of data.

The growth in raw data as a source of information bodes well for data scientists. But there is more. Glassdor (https://www.glassdoor.com) lists Data Science as third on its list of 50 best occupations (2022). Discussed at the top of this chapter are projections from the U.S. Bureau of Labor Statistics (US BLS) Occupational Outlook Handbook, which also presents good news.[8]

Other sources only confirm what we can infer from the rapid growth in data sources and from what we see at Glassdoor, the US BLS, and other similar sources. According to data from the Institute of Electrical and Electronics Engineers (IEEE), the U.S. Bureau of Labor Statistics may be understating potential earnings in data science. A 2021 survey by IEEE estimates the median salary in data science at $164,500 per year.

Howard University, University of Connecticut, and University of California San Diego have announced new master's degree programs since the start of 2022, demonstrating the potential growth in the field of data science education (Griset, 2022). A brief search online reveals more schools with degrees or certificate programs in data science, including the University of Wisconsin-Madison, Northwestern University, Cornell University, and East Carolina University.

---

[8] Reminder: This statistic is based on a position called "computer and information research scientists" (the handbook's best euphemism for data science). Persons in this role earn a median annual income of $131,490. In other words, data scientists potentially earn almost three times the median annual income of "all occupations."

Data science education is not just growing in the United States. We know this because Gizmodo (and others) have recently listed dozens of top universities now offering degrees (undergraduate or graduate) in data science across the globe (Gizmodo, 2022). I am certain that every list misses at least a few important examples. Canadian Occupational Projection Systems has made a long-term projection that data scientists will be in high demand through 2029, the end of their forecast, with immigrants and foreign students filling a gap for desired workers (Government of Canada Job Bank, 2022). Canada's policies are friendly toward international students, making it a top destination for those seeking the qualifications to work in the public and private sectors (Gupta, 2022).

Another factor about the future of data science that weighs in favor of this field as a career choice for those looking to make a career transition is that the hard-earned and costly-to-obtain skills in data science are highly transferable. Your skills in statistics and programming will continue to support your career opportunities even later in your career, if you should decide not to stay specifically in data science.

Technology and methods are continually improving. Data scientists must keep current on a broad set of modern technologies in order to be well-positioned for future career pivots. A broad set of skills and technical competencies in a data-driven environment means employers may seek out data scientists for other positions at a range of companies.

A globally high demand for data scientists expands your list of options when choosing where you will live and work. For example, citizens of the E.U. can choose their place of work within the E.U., as they can access employment in any other member state. This means a data scientist can readily work in Munich, Berlin, Paris, Amsterdam, Hamburg, or Frankfurt, which were all listed as the top European cities to live and work for data scientists in 2019 (European Leadership University, 2019). Data science job postings in the U.K. have grown 1,287% from 2013–2018 (The Royal Society, 2019).

The "Typical" Data Scientist

Here is the truth. There is no "typical" data scientist. Just as there is no really "typical" profile of a mid- or late-career professional. I put the word *typical* in quotation marks because as a word choice, it is a compromise.

I have briefly mentioned Daveed, Poleh, and Jodi. I explained that they are hypothetical data scientists who leveraged deep knowledge from their business domains in order to facilitate their transitions into data science. In this section, I further introduce these three characters, who are each unique data scientists from diverse backgrounds. While reading about their experiences, you may further explore what it means to be a mid- or late-career professional with an interest in data science.

Consider how their careers added to their skills, abilities, and experiences in administration, management, supervision, strategy, and leadership. Consider how they offer assets related to their professional networks. Lastly, consider the credibility they have acquired as mid- or late-career professionals.

Be sure to think through how their distinct paths unfolded into successful data science positions. Each profile includes a discussion related to their *why*, which was the topic of this book's introduction.

This section on Daveed, Poleh, and Jodi is not a section that means to define for you the skills and abilities of a data scientist. The above sections defined those skills and abilities for you. Instead, note both the personal and professional experiences that mid- and late-career professionals bring with them, experiences which other professionals do not necessarily have in the same measure. It is important for mid- and late-career professionals who are in the midst of a career transition to understand how these experiences differentiate themselves from others on the job search, especially those who are applying for similar positions.

Daveed (or Dav but does not prefer Dave)
Dav sounds like "have" but starts with a D
Pronouns: ze/zim/zis

Daveed became a data scientist after years of working in primary and secondary education.

In the 1990s throughout the United States, primary and secondary schools tracked students for particular transitions after high school graduation. Students were prepared for a specific post-graduation path by being sorted into tracks. Roughly speaking, those paths included: directly entering the workforce, attending technical school before beginning a technical career, or entering a 4-year collegiate program. Daveed's high school did not track zim for college. Daveed's academic performance in high school was mixed. Ze earned low or modest grades in math and language, but did very well in science and foreign languages. Therefore, Daveed lacked the necessary preparation for college after graduation. With guidance from community-based mentors, Daveed learned about opportunities to teach English abroad.

Daveed attended a certification program that prepared zim to teach English as a foreign language (TEFL). With modest savings that Daveed had accumulated during high school, plus support from his mentors, Daveed completed the TEFL certification and taught English in Budapest, Hungary for a year after high school. Daveed's parents could not offer financial support during the time ze was abroad.

After living and working abroad, Daveed attended college and then worked in higher education administration. Later, Daveed transitioned into a short-term retail career where ze managed an automobile rental center. Eventually, Daveed decided ze wanted to further pursue zis career in higher education, specifically to work with developing and enforcing policies at colleges and universities. The desire to work in higher education led Daveed to attend and graduate law school. For 6 years following law school, Daveed worked in higher education and then returned to school and completed a PhD.

Throughout the PhD program, Daveed began working with advanced analytics, statistics, data analysis, and data science. The experience and skills Daveed acquired in advanced analytics, statistics, data analysis, and data science (as a part of zis graduate program) eventually led zim to pursue a career in data science.

Currently, Daveed works for a large international consulting firm that serves government, non-profit, and corporate clients. Daveed works for a practice area within zis firm that contributes to projects with multiple clients (primarily governmental clients, including boards of education and large public university systems).

Daveed's *why* is to help others succeed. Zis source of motivation for working in data science is the opportunity to study social and cultural outcomes by race, class, gender, nationality, religion, and socio-economic status. Daveed shares a passion common to many data scientists: generating and disseminating new knowledge about how the world works. Daveed further desires to focus on understanding how and why individuals are able (or unable) to: start and finish college, achieve success in a career, and remain healthy.

At times in zis career, Daveed has both simultaneously underestimated zis own capabilities while also feeling underestimated by those around zim. Others in Daveed's work and personal life view zim as highly capable. On more than one occasion, prospective employers have suggested to zim that ze was overqualified for the roles ze sought.

Poleh, which sounds like "Paula"
Often goes by Pol, which sounds like "Paul"
Pronouns: she/her/hers

With some encouragement from extended family (who also worked in data science), Poleh became a data scientist after she had spent an extended portion of her career as a marketing director at an electronic medical records (EMR) software firm.

As a high school student, Poleh did well in math and science. However, schools limited computer education for students, especially for girls and young women, in the 1980s and 1990s. She remembers taking (and enjoying) a typing class in high school—on a typewriter. Poleh considers herself a "technology immigrant." She wears the moniker as a badge of honor. Poleh knows that being a technology immigrant while simultaneously working at the front edge of technology (through a career in data science) distinguishes her from many of her younger colleagues who are technology "natives." In her early years, Poleh learned how to navigate life without the constant presence of technology, and later she needed to incorporate technology into her work and professional life. This experience has brought her a healthy skepticism for technology in general, and more specifically, for data analysis. This skepticism fits her personality. She embraces innovation in her professional career, but she can be the most difficult to persuade that a new technology will serve her team or organization well. Her healthy skepticism is useful to her employers and co-workers. They know that Poleh's critical eye saves the team from moving too quickly or too soon in directions that could be detrimental to long-term success.

Poleh attended high school in New York, received a liberal arts college education in Virginia, and then completed graduate school in Georgia (obtaining a degree in information technology management). Her favorite semester in college was the semester she studied abroad in France.

Shortly after undergrad, Poleh worked in real estate sales. She split her time working a salaried role in rental property management and a commissioned-based role selling real estate as an agent. After approximately 5 years in sales, Poleh transitioned into project management in the field of information technology. Right before graduate school, Poleh transitioned into a role that involved supporting installation and maintenance of

EMR software. After graduate school, Poleh continued working for EMR software firms but transitioned into roles related to marketing. Poleh learned that the advanced analytical skills necessary for success as a marketing leader would support a transition into data science. She also saw the potential to leverage her domain knowledge as a specialist in EMR software into practicing data scientist. When the EMR firms cut back on marketing personnel, Poleh took the opportunity to transition into data science.

Poleh's *why* is her dedication to ensuring the next generation will have the opportunities that were not yet available when Poleh was younger. This dedication applies generally to all children and especially to Poleh's own child. Unlike Dav, who incorporated aspects of zis intrinsic sources of motivation into zis professional role, Poleh is pragmatic about her approach to career progression. She has pursued advancement in her career so that she can provide for herself and her family. She is proud of her career, yet she is confident that she would have been happy in other lines of work too. Her happiness comes from having work that lets her focus ample personal time and energy on her family.

In her personal time, she loves to be with family. Poleh is married with one child, and she is close with both her own parents and her in-laws. Her child's hobbies are Poleh's hobbies. She also enjoys taking classes (cooking classes, painting classes, gym classes—anything that allows her to learn new things).

She is happy with her life and career. At times, she is self-conscious about having transitioned careers multiple times.

However, she has accepted her path as a form of diversity that gives her strength. Most people in her professional and personal life describe her as polished, agreeable, and flexible. She feels, and most agree with her, that she can fit in anyplace.

A nuance of Poleh's later career transitions is that while she changed her professional role many times (from sales, then to technical support and implementation, on to marketing, and finally into data science), she has primarily remained within the same industry. Poleh is sometimes an overthinker, which can be both advantageous and disadvantageous. For example, even though she often dwells on self-conscious thoughts related to having changed careers many times, she can quickly remind herself that she has focused primarily in one industry. She can also remind herself that there are few other professionals with a knowledge of EMR software as broad and as rich as hers.

Poleh continues her career within the EMR software industry but as a data scientist.

Jodi, who goes by Jodi
Pronouns: they/them/their(s)

After working as a research associate, Jodi eventually transitioned into data science because Jodi had already effectively been working as a data scientist, albeit informally. Working formally as a data scientist provided better pay.

For Jodi, informally working as a data scientist meant doing the work of a data scientist but without the title, compensation, or other associated returns. Formally working as a data scientist meant finding a job that would allow them to be specifically responsible for executing projects that involve data science work.

Jodi was born in Cameroon and then raised primarily in Canada. They attended elementary and middle school primarily in Canada. Jodi is fluent in French and English. However, Jodi graduated high school in the United States in the 1990s. As an undergrad at a state-supported public university in the United States, Jodi studied sociology. Jodi switched to psychology for their master's degree. They took no breaks between high school, college, or graduate school, and so they finished their master's degree at the age of 24. Jodi also worked part time on a PhD; they had began collecting data but then lost funding for school and elected not to finish the program.

During college and graduate school, Jodi worked as a barista at a popular national coffee chain. While working for the coffee chain, Jodi earned a range of the company's regional awards for employees who learned about coffee history, origins, production, preparation, and business. The coffee chain would have liked Jodi to continue working for them. Jodi considered the opportunities that the coffee chain may have offered long term. The reason Jodi had chosen sociology and psychology was because they had believed those choices would support a career in academia. Since a career in academia did not unfold in the way Jodi had originally expected that it would, Jodi needed to consider other career options.

Ultimately, Jodi felt pressure from family to disregard career options in the coffee industry. Much of Jodi's family implied that it would not bring sufficient prestige. Despite an interest in career options within the coffee industry, Jodi succumbed to social pressure urging them to "use their college and graduate degrees." Jodi perceived that their friends and family pressured them to forgo opportunities in coffee because the coffee career would mean "wasting their degrees in sociology and psychology." Right after graduate school, Jodi worked as a policy research associate for a pharmaceutical corporation. Jodi was happy that the pharmaceutical work drew heavily upon their academic training while simultaneously garnering family approval. Their work involved reviewing research related to health disparities, and Jodi's educational background in sociology and psychology supported this work. To effectively analyze the data related to health disparities, Jodi's company provided training and development opportunities in Python, R, and SAS.

After a successful transition into data science while remaining within the pharmaceutical industry, Jodi later changed industries. As a data scientist, Jodi has worked in politics, serving within a team of scientists who supported national election campaigns. They expanded their network in politics, enduring the highs and lows of political campaign work. Jodi then continued their data science work but for regional and national non-profit organizations. At present, their specialty is working with data related to the educational outcomes of trans and immigrant children throughout North America.

Jodi's parents worked as consultants in the mining industry. As a result, Jodi frequently moved when they were young. Jodi married right out of college, then divorced less than a year later without having children. They later transitioned from female to male.

Jodi's *why* is their devotion to setting a good example for their younger siblings. They also seek opportunities that will allow them to contribute to their sibling's education. And, as a trans immigrant, Jodi desires to help other immigrants find opportunities that have been previously unavailable to members of the trans and immigrant communities.

Both in Jodi's personal and professional life, they are extremely independent. After Jodi graduated high school, Jodi's parents moved away for the next consulting gig. Jodi stayed behind for college to benefit from the in-state tuition, and they also remained in the United States for graduate school. Except for a brief marriage, Jodi has lived alone (or with roommates) since graduating high school.

***

Later in this book, I write more about Daveed, Poleh, and Jodi. I am so happy to share these characters with you because until I began writing this book, they lived only in my mind. Now they will live in your mind too. To help you know and understand these characters more fully, I have invented personal, professional, familial, and social characteristics that I believe to be at least somewhat representative of the range of professionals I have known from my own experiences. I hope these three characters will be a source of inspiration for you as they have been for me.

As you grow acquainted with Daveed, Poleh, and Jodi, do as I have and start to count them as new friends. I rely on these three characters when I make decisions about my career. They serve as a source of advice (to complement the advice I also get from real people).

I intend for these characters to help you understand the kinds of people who might pursue a career in data science.

The short version is that data science is a meaningful path for a diverse range of people.

Above and beyond their pragmatic roles in this book, these three characters are now your new friends too. They care about you and your success. Let them guide you.

Chapter Summary

As a profession, data science is an interdisciplinary area of practice and research involving scientific processes, advanced mathematics, computer programming, statistics, data mining, text processing, and other related notions. The field requires professionals who can operate within this interdisciplinary setting. I argued in this chapter that mid- and late-career professionals bring a measure of interdisciplinary experiences with them that other younger professionals often have not yet acquired.

Mid- and late-career professionals have acquired domain knowledge from their past work experiences, which gives them strong potential as data scientists. This strong potential stems, at least in part, from a demonstrated ability to solve industry-specific problems.

There is a skills gap in the data science industry, in both education (as data science degrees are relatively new) and knowledge. For those who are willing to make the efforts and investments necessary to transition careers, this gap presents an opportunity for mid- and late-career professionals to advance their careers by transitioning into data science. Possession of domain knowledge is one way in which mid- and late-career professionals can help close these gaps in the field.

In this chapter, I wrote about how a data scientist should possess a series of traits that may include:

➢ A curious mind.
➢ An instinct for finding, recognizing, and explaining patterns.
➢ Patience.
➢ An interest and familiarity with process design / development.
➢ A love for data, technology, and communication.

Growth rates and salaries in the field of data science are predicted to increase from 2020 to 2030. Although the field is growing rapidly, data science is not a new line of work. In fact, some may trace the origin of data science back to the 1800s, through the work of Ada Lovelace. Even though she was never officially labeled a data scientist, she wrote and worked as one. I value Ada's story because she exemplifies an important aspect of data science, that the field is open to anyone willing to work for it.

This chapter discussed how and why moving into data science continues to leave open other career options even later in a mid- or late-career professional's future. The skills acquired in working as a data scientist are highly transferable.

An important take-away is that by keeping current on a broad set of technologies, you will be well-positioned for future career pivots. Others may seek you out for career opportunities alongside data science due to your overall set of skills and technical competencies in a data-driven environment.

Lastly, to reintroduce the notion that there is no "typical" data scientist, this chapter introduced you to three fictional data scientists. When this book is over, you will know these three friends well enough to ask yourself: *I wonder what Jodi might say or do in this situation?* By asking and imagining how Daveed, Poleh, or Jodi would behave in any situation, you will have a helpful source of insight on how you might proceed in an uncertain scenario.

CHAPTER 3

You Might Already Be a Data Scientist

There are data scientists who have yet to earn a living as data scientists. This chapter is about discovering if you may be in this category of folks. While evaluating your current role, this chapter will look at if and when you should seek additional training. Importantly, this chapter will address the phenomena of imposter syndrome. Additional training and professional development is a given for data science professionals. However, this chapter will explain how additional training is not a cure for imposter syndrome. When you do pursue additional training, this chapter also gives advice on how you can maximize the return on investment associated with that additional training and professional development.

In the previous chapter, I introduced you to Ada Lovelace. Imagine a modern 2020s Ada Lovelace. Ask yourself, *What would Ada Lovelace call herself today if she were alive?* My money is on her calling herself a data scientist—even though she never completed a degree in data science nor a data science bootcamp. Despite the fact that she never held a position with the job title of data scientist and despite all of Ada's "resume gaps," Ada would call herself a data scientist (in my imagination). And I say good for Ada because it is a lucrative career option, and it also happens to call on a set of skills she can perform well.

Imagine how the history of science, computers, and data analysis might have been different if Ada Lovelace had let self-doubt or a lack of external validation stall or delay her professional advancements. As she was the first programmer, the subsequent advances in technology may have stalled for years or decades without her. I hope you will let Lovelace's story be a source of inspiration for you.

Somewhat like Ada, Jodi was working as a data scientist in an informal sense. Jodi decided to transition into a data science career when they realized that largely, they were already working as a data scientist. Jodi decided they deserved the additional career development, advancement, and salary options that came with formally being in a data science role.

Before you can convince others that you are a data scientist, there are two necessary conditions. First, it must be true. Second, you have to convince yourself it is true. In my experience, the second does not necessarily follow the first. Here, I provide words of wisdom as you not only shift your career but also shift your sense of who you are as a professional.

We often intertwine our identity with our work. It feels like a daily occurrence that I meet professionals who are already working as data scientists but because they are trained for another role, they are reluctant to take the title of data scientist. The ultimate purpose of this section is to help readers shift their mindset and drop any reluctance that may hold them back from claiming the title of data scientist (even before getting that first data science job).

There is a difference between *being* a data scientist and *earning a living as* a data scientist. The same goes for many pursuits in life. For example, there is a difference between being an athlete and *earning a living as* an athlete. Further, for those familiar with the world of professional athleticism, there is a difference between working as a *professional* athlete and *earning a living as* an athlete.

To elaborate: Many professional athletes do not earn an income sufficient to support themselves and their family solely through professional athletic income sources such as sponsorships. This means we need to be more precise with our language. This book aims to help mid- and late-career professionals transition into paid roles that will allow you to *earn a living as* a data scientist. Many readers may already be data scientists, but they may not yet be earning a living in a role that their employer regards as data science.

Unlike the exclusive world of professional athleticism, data science is a world that is open to many professionals. This chapter aims to help you assess if you already operate as a data scientist and if you already possess the skills and abilities necessary to call yourself a data scientist. Essentially, if you operate as a data scientist and if you possess the skills and abilities necessary to call yourself a data scientist, then you are a data scientist. Step one in the process of making that transition is done.

The next step will be to transition into a role that will allow you to earn a living as a data scientist. In other words, find a role working for an employer or a client that will allow you to support yourself and your family while working as a data scientist.

Your Job (Title) Does Not Define You

I have learned that my job title does not define who I am as a person. Unfortunately, this is a lesson I did not learn until late in life. Sometimes, your job title does not even properly define your role at work. Learning these hard-to-absorb truths held me back from advancing my career. I was working for a large university within the division of enrollment management, which concerned itself with student recruitment, course registration, student and course records, and the institution's distribution of financial aid and awards. From an empirical perspective, this position involved interacting with some of the most interesting data any data scientist could hope to work with.

My employer's human resources database did not call me a data scientist. I was a divisional policy advisor (or some other similar iteration I long ago jettisoned from my permanent memory).

However, in this policy advisor role, I implemented many analyses and projects that used advanced analytic techniques. One of my projects was to predict which students may be at risk of not performing as well as expected. I approached this problem with logistic regression, decision trees, and k-nearest neighbors. You see, I was performing data science.

I was not the first to call myself a data scientist. When I told my professional associates (who were data scientists) about my work, they started calling me a data scientist. A major turn of events in my understanding and confidence was when my supervisor started calling me a data scientist. My supervisor did not change my title, in a formal sense, but conversationally, I became known as the office's data scientist.

Imposter Syndrome Is Real

When my colleagues began regarding me as a data scientist, I initially deflected and demurred—I felt like an imposter. I felt like a literal (not figurative) imposter. I naggingly thought to myself, *I can not be a data scientist.*

A partial list of reasons that made me reluctant to accept myself as a data scientist:

- I did not have a degree in data science (*although I had a PhD*).

- I did not have a degree in computer science (*although I had been in school for more than half of my life*).
- I did not have a degree in statistics (*although I had experience in teaching statistics*).
- Human resources did not regard me as a data scientist (*although everyone who knew me well at work was calling me a data scientist*).

In hindsight, I readily reminded myself of the items on this list of personal deficits. These self-reminders were manifestations of imposter syndrome.

When you are looking for a job, it is easy to feel like you are not good enough. You might think that you cannot do the job as well as someone with a more traditional background. This happened to me when I was looking for a job as a data scientist. Another thing that can happen is that you might not be very clear about your goals or what you want in a job. I experienced that lack of clarity and confusion when influential members of my community started referring to me as a data scientist, even though I was not initially aiming for that career. Another sinister portion of this curse is that you can spend too much time looking at jobs that are very safe. So-called "safe" jobs are those for which you have more than all the qualifications. It is not uncommon for prospective employers to tell those who suffer from imposter syndrome, "We feel you are overqualified." A good example of this is Dav, who had been told many times by prospective employers that they felt ze was overqualified for the roles ze sought.

Imposter syndrome is a form of self-doubt. It is a temptation (or for some, a powerful instinct) to count your own achievements and successes as the result of luck—or even the result of a fluke or a mistake. Negative self-talk is a characteristic of imposter syndrome. Counterintuitively, high achievers often experience imposter syndrome. Imposter syndrome is not logical or reasonable.

If you do not learn to identify and then beat imposter syndrome, it can prevent you from achieving further success. Worse, you will continue to produce quality work for others while not demanding fair compensation for the value you bring. Despite the lack of logic and reason, imposter syndrome is a common and normal experience (Sakulku and Alexander, 2011).[9]

Imposter syndrome is also measurable. The research scientists who first identified, studied, and wrote about this phenomenon developed a scale. This imposter syndrome measurement scale is known as the Clance IP Scale, after its namesake creator, Pauline Clance.

The good news is that there are at least two tactics you can use to minimize the influence imposter syndrome has on your mind and on your career.

---

[9] I recommend reading Dr. Lisa Orbé-Austin's book, *Own Your Greatness: Overcome Imposter Syndrom, Beat Self-Doubt, and Succeed in Life.*

Be Clear on What You Want

This is the first of a handful of imposter syndrome antidotes I often point others toward. Once you are clear on what you want, you can begin building confidence around that specific and clear career objective.

In addition to all the reasons listed above, another worry haunted me. Did I even want to be a data scientist? I had recently completed a PhD in educational leadership and policy analysis. Following the PhD program, I wanted to work as an academic. I wanted to be a researcher and a teacher. I wanted to work as a faculty member at a college or university. I wanted to do what a course in PhD study trains and prepares you to do. Moreover, many of the most influential and helpful supporters in my life at the time also wanted these things for me.

In earnest, however, I knew that data science might be a more lucrative and an equally fulfilling career option. For example, I would still get to teach. I have had the pleasure of teaching for many universities. I also teach often in corporate training seminars. I knew that the skills and abilities I had acquired through the PhD program would apply well to a career in data science.

In hindsight, I know what really held me back was imposter syndrome. If you are worried that pursuing a career in data science might limit your ability to continue with other things you love, my experience shows that you will find a way to keep the things you really love in your life.

For example, Dav has continued to do work that aligns with zis passion for helping students learn. The difference is that, as a data scientist, ze helps students on a larger scale, through working with clients who serve hundreds or thousands of students at a time. In this way, Dav's work as a data scientist is at least as impactful as zis work was in the classroom.

Poleh's motivations in life differ from her friend Dav. Poleh is hyper-focused on her family. During her transition, she needed to focus more on her career and her job search. Poleh worked hard, largely within a specific industry, but now that she has settled into her career as a data scientist and plans to remain in this career, she can enjoy her hobbies too (and her kid's hobbies).

Perhaps more than Dav and Poleh combined, Jodi felt pressure from friends, family, mentors, and supporters to pursue a career in sociology and psychology, even though a career in the coffee industry enticed them. Eventually, Jodi transitioned into data science, and they realized an important dynamic. Jodi's friends, family, mentors, and supporters wanted Jodi to be happy and prosperous. Once Jodi found a sense of clarity regarding a career track that really made sense for them, all of Jodi's friends, family, mentors, and supporters rallied for that cause.

By being clear with yourself and others that you aim to be a data scientist, you will undo at least some of the imposter syndrome symptoms you may experience. Being clear on what you want will help you leverage the advice I offer in other portions of this book. For example, in Chapter 4, I write extensively about preparing your friends and family for your transition. Without having first decided that you wish to work as a data scientist, it is difficult to communicate that desire to friends and family. For another example, it is vital to convey a specific career purpose and objective when speaking with recruiters because they are eager to work with candidates who have decided on a specific career path.

The Upside and Downside to Additional Training

Another appealing though frequently counterproductive "cure" for imposter syndrome is to seek additional training. This so-called "cure" can be problematic because it does not always solve imposter syndrome. Sometimes, additional training can even make imposter syndrome worse. Therefore, avoid seeking additional training solely as a response to feelings of imposter syndrome.

Over time, all data scientists will acquire additional knowledge, skills, and abilities through additional training. This additional training is essential for staying current and up to date in the field. Learning new techniques is an important aspect of ensuring you can serve a diverse range of clients well. A broad repertoire will allow you to bring the best method to resolving your client's concerns and business problems. As discussed in Chapter 2, a love and passion for learning new things is a trait common among data science professionals. Fulfilling your desire to learn new things is an upside to choosing data science as a career path.

However, there are also downsides to seeking additional training. The downsides are that gaining additional knowledge, skills, and abilities requires time, energy, and resources. There is an opportunity cost: You could spend the required time, energy, and resources on other investments instead. Training may have a financial cost as well. To be clear, the time spent on acquiring additional knowledge, skills, and abilities is not insignificant. I spend a few weeks a year on this. The costs add up—books, Udemy courses, Udacity courses, LinkedIn Learning, the occasional weekend workshop, or a national training seminar. Sometimes, work will pay for these or give you time to work on these, but not always. Be sure to keep this demand on your time, energy, and resources in mind as you proceed in this career. Data scientists must plan for these demands on their time, energy, and resources.

To help manage decisions related to pursuing new training, this section advises on when and how to seek additional training. In addition, this section offers advice on how to maximize your learning when you do attend additional courses.

My advice to anyone considering more courses, certifications, degrees, or bootcamps is to consider whether the urge to do this is the result of imposter syndrome. Taking more classes and gaining more credentials can devolve into a self-reinforcing trap that will limit your ability to transition to a role in which you can earn a living as a data scientist.

As long as you are pursuing added training for the sake of expanding your skills, not to beat imposter syndrome, the final portion of this chapter advises you on how you can maximize the return on investment that added training can provide for your career.

How to Maximize the Training Return on Investment

A preliminary step you should consider is to obtain a measurement of your existing skills. Usually, the best way to measure your existing skills objectively is to take a quiz designed to assess your current level. Doing this kind of assessment before diving into a new course or resource will aid you in identifying gaps in your knowledge, so you can target specific areas for improvement. DataLemur (https://datalemur.com) helps you to evaluate your existing knowledge of SQL and then build on that knowledge. Other sites that can objectively assess your coding and technical skills with practice exams or quizzes beyond SQL include but are not limited to: 365 Data (https://365datascience.com), Data Camp (https://www.datacamp.com), Analytics Vidhya (https://datahack.analyticsvidhya.com), and Skillsoft (https://www.skillsoft.com). Remember that any assessment has weaknesses and limitations. Low performance on any one assessment should not be a deterrent.

With the vast array of resources and courses available, it can be difficult to determine which will provide the most bang for your buck. When reviewing a potential course, choose the course in which you can invest the most time, energy, and thought. You will get out of the course what you put into the course. Use the guidelines and advice that follow to ensure that you make an effort equal to the value you hope for on your return on investment.

Take Notes

Start for yourself a note-taking system. Many mid- and late-career professionals will be familiar with the process of taking notes with pen and paper during in-person classes, where the instructor stands in front of a group and delivers information. As training increasingly moves to an online learning environment, it can feel less formal. In this informal setting, it is tempting for many to skip taking notes.

Because one of the benefits of online learning is that you can review the original material (recorded lectures, demonstrations, and on-demand resources) at a later date, it may seem that taking notes is unnecessary. However, taking notes is essential.

Taking notes assists you in building and retaining new knowledge. While there are plenty of apps and online tools available to help you take notes, there is evidence that you learn best when you actually write notes on paper. Taking notes increases both comprehension and retention. It also helps you learn to organize ideas and key concepts while providing a personalized resource for your review.

That being said, studies have found that taking notes on a computer has certain advantages. For one, since you typically type faster than you write, it is possible to record more words. Students tend to type an instructor's statements verbatim, rather than a handwritten summary of what the instructor said.

A benefit of long-hand note-taking is better focus. It is harder to put your pen down and scroll your social media feed, for example. Improved retention is another benefit associated with taking notes by hand: The act of listening and then condensing and summarizing material helps students process material and retain it better.

I recommend taking notes by hand. Then, type them up later on. I base this advice on the persuasive research on this topic (Doubek, 2016). Plus, that is how I do it.

Use Learning Platform Q&A

Most platforms have a Q&A section. As an instructor, I monitor the Q&A board in my Udemy, Canvas, Kajabi, and other course platforms. The Q&A section is a good place to get more support, but it is also a helpful place to flag material that needs clarification. Often, instructors will update their courses based on discussions in the Q&A.

Many people treat Q&A as an afterthought. This is both a missed learning opportunity and a missed relationship-building opportunity. Different learning platforms will have different Q&A styles. No matter what online platform you are using, the Q&A section can be a valuable learning tool for students.

Some will skip the Q&A because of social anxiety, shyness, or a lack of confidence. If you have a question, chances are others will too. First, search the Q&A to see if someone has already asked your question (and it has been answered). But after that step, I suggest you dive in.

Additional advice I want you to follow is to treat everyone with respect. It can be easy to mistreat others. A good start is to avoid addressing others in the class, on the discussion board or in other venues, at the beginning of your question with the words "hey guys." (Nelson, 2020e).

Use Captions (Where Available)

Thanks to advances in data science, captions are increasingly available on video and audio content. Make sure you turn the captions on whenever you are watching online instructional videos. Reading the captions (while watching and listening to the instructor) will improve your ability to build and retain new knowledge.

Enabling the captions will provide a richer experience too. Whether or not you know it, when you are watching and listening to an instructional video, your brain is only capable of processing a portion of the material. By adding the words to the screen, your brain can more easily access the material and fully process it.

Reading captions is particularly beneficial to students whose first language is not the language of instruction and for those with learning impairments, like myself. We also have scientific evidence that confirms the benefits of reading captions while simultaneously listening and watching.

Using captions can improve testing results, enhance recall, deepen processing, and lead to better engagement. Using captions may result in a more positive attitude toward the material. This will enhance comprehension and boost memory (Jae, 2019).

Use Video Speed Selectors

This bit of advice applies to prerecorded, on-demand, instructional content. The feature works in at least two ways. You can increase the speed when there is material you already know. Likewise, you can decrease the speed when you need a deeper focus.

Most video players have a speed selector, which allows the viewer to slow the playback or speed it up. Use this feature to your advantage. When the instructor is covering material you already know well, speed the playback to 1.5x or 2x to save time. When you are not as familiar with the material, or want to take more complete notes, slow the playback to 0.75x or 0.5x.

Speeding video playback allows you to consume more material in up to half the amount of time. You can view a 40-minute video played at 2x in just 20 minutes. Drawbacks include mental exhaustion and possibly misremembering the material at a later date. It may take some experimentation to find the speed that is best for you.

Chapter Summary

This chapter, and the book thus far, has likely led you to go within and ask yourself some deep questions. You have begun to consider whether you are in fact already a data scientist, why you may struggle with self-identifying as one, and how imposter syndrome may influence your future career in data science. This chapter also examined how many professionals with the desire to be a data scientist but with one or more perceived gaps in their skills or experiences may be tempted to focus too much on seeking additional training.

Remember to be clear on what you want (and how a career in data science will achieve this for you). Being confident in your career goals should help to dispel feelings of imposter syndrome. A confident sense of direction is crucial when speaking with recruiters as well. Lastly, a confident sense of direction will make it easier for people in your life to support you during your transition, which is an important topic of the chapter ahead.

Imposter syndrome can lead mid- and late-career professionals to believe that more education or training will make them more qualified. Counterintuitively, my advice to anyone considering more courses, certifications, degrees, or bootcamps is to consider whether the urge to take more courses or gain more credentials might actually be the result of imposter syndrome.

You will never know everything there is to know. Understanding that there is always going to be something to learn will allow you to refocus your energy on landing your next amazing data science role. However, when you do find that you need to pursue added training, follow this chapter's advice on making the best of the learning experience, such as taking notes, visiting the Q&A section on a learning platform, using instructional video captions, and using instructional video speed selections.

> You are more ready than you think you are!
>
> @adamrossnelson

Please Rate + Review

Your book ratings and your reviews matter!

Adam Ross Nelson

More Information: https://coaching.adamrossnelson.com/

CHAPTER 4

Preparing Friends, Family, and Others for Your Career Transition

On top of providing an overview of how and why this chapter's steps require extra consideration for many mid- and late-career professionals, this chapter will revisit many of the reasons mid- and late-career professionals look to transition.

Mid- and late-career professionals have a family dynamic that many early-career professionals might not have. For example, mid- and late-career professionals may have spouses (current or former). Mid- and late-career professionals are more likely to have children who are old enough to understand and be sensitive to a parent's change in career. Some mid- and late-career professionals may currently be working to help children in establishing or starting their own careers. Helping your kids prepare for their career while simultaneously starting a new career of your own is a unique challenge.

As discussed in earlier chapters, the professional network mid- and late-career professionals bring with them is an asset. Like most assets, this professional network requires maintenance. For reasons discussed in this chapter, it is important for mid- and late-career professionals to maintain their professional network over time and then prepare that network in anticipation of a career transition.

In order to complete a career transition as a mid- or late-career professional, we need to face the often unspoken dynamic that we must be vulnerable to our friends, family, and professional network. You will need to announce to everyone who has supported you that you no longer wish to be in the place they helped you reach.

Making this kind of announcement may seem to imply, consciously or unconsciously, that you have grown ungrateful for the help and support that got you where you are. On a related note, many of the people who helped and supported you in advancing to where you are now will be in a similar place in life, as it is not uncommon for us to emulate our supporters, supervisors, co-workers, and mentors. Oftentimes, our mentors invested time and energy into helping us achieve a kind of success that resembles their own. Again, making a significant career change announcement may seem to suggest, consciously or unconsciously, a rejection or criticism of those supporters and their choices. The risk is that your decision will imply that you no longer find your role (which may be similar to your mentors' roles) to be fulfilling—or worse, worthy of your interests and abilities.

If neglected, the steps associated with preparing friends and family for your career transition can inhibit your ability to transition. If cultivated, the steps associated with preparing friends and family for your career transition can propel the transition.

The Case for Empathy

It is possible that some who are close to you will feel a sense of hesitation given your career change. Remember though that their feelings are valid. In many cases, these feelings are about them and their struggles. Be empathetic to those who might second-guess your choice but remain firm in your decision. Others who depend on you might think moving into data science is the wrong move to make. Ultimately, it is your move to make. It is your leap to leap.

Throughout the course of the transition, you simultaneously need to honor your existing associations while also finding and growing new associations. You need to find, recruit, nurture, and announce to an entire new cohort of supporters and helpers that you are interested in joining a new field.

When introducing yourself to this new cohort, the conscious or unconscious fear is that you will have to respond to that new cohort's skepticism. Addressing that skepticism would come as justifying why you "waited" until later in your life to pursue this work, while their devotion to this career formed earlier in life and has remained constant. The unflattering implication is that you once thought this alternative career path was not good enough for you, but now, perhaps due to vanity or opportunism, you suddenly are interested.

In more specific terms, many mid- and late-career professionals have relied on help and support from others. For example, very early in our careers, we had teachers and professors who served as references for us. Those teachers and professors taught us, from within the context of a classroom, how to do our work. They passed their knowledge, skills, and expertise on to us.

For another example, many mid- and late-career professionals may have benefited from the support of former supervisors and co-workers. Those former supervisors and co-workers mentored and guided us on our way to where we are now. As we grew our career and applied for new positions, those supervisors and co-workers wrote recommendations and served as references for us. Maybe they showed us job listings and opportunities about which we might not have known otherwise.

Given the supportive community we built on our way to mid- or late-career status, we value those who have helped us along the way. Of course, we want to honor and respect their contributions to our career success.

We have family who have helped us along the way. Our children are proud of us (whether or not they will admit it). Our parents might think we are in charge of our entire organization (or professional field) and then wonder why we want to forsake that (perceived) prestige. Our partners lovingly took up slack at home when we were finishing our certifications, degrees, bootcamps, and other educational accomplishments.

Of course, we helped others along the way, too. The support has been mutual. But, without the help and support of others, we would not be where we are now.

This support is one reason many mid- and late-career professionals may hesitate to pursue major career transitions. Leaving our current line of work may seem to imply a lack of respect or appreciation for the help and support others have offered us in our career. In other words, the worry and hesitation could be because you feel you are risking alienation of or from your existing supporters.

A major career change means facing the prospect of skepticism from future supporters and helpers. The prospect of replicating or adding to our personal and professional network of support is also intimidating , which leads to additional hesitation.

Fear & Hesitation's Antidote

This fear and hesitation have an antidote. The antidote is to remember that those who supported you gave their support not because they wanted you to enter whatever professional role you are in now. Sure, in some cases, they once aided you in pursuing careers that mirrored their own careers. There were teachers, professors, and former supervisors who helped you succeed by helping you emulate their work. Of course, those teachers, professors, and former supervisors were happy to see you succeed in lines of work similar to their own.

But nobody wanted you to pursue your earlier career choices because they wanted you to be more like them. They wanted you to pursue your earlier career choices because they wanted you to be you. Everyone who was there for you along your way did so in service of helping you be you.

Because your existing network wants you to be you, they will not take your decision to change careers as an indication that you are unthankful. The opposite will happen. They will take your decision to change careers as one more reason to celebrate you and who you are. Your friends and family will recognize your new direction as a continuing devotion to your own career and success. Pursuing these transitions evidence a growth mindset.

This extensive personal network on which mid- and late-career professionals have relied is an asset we bring with us when we transition careers. Prospective employers need to understand, and we need to communicate, the value of this network. The same network that helped and supported us in our earlier success will still be available to help and support us in our new lines of work. That political and social capital will benefit us, and we can leverage it to benefit our new employers— and the causes about which our new employers care.

Reasons for Change

As you will see later in this section, I group most motivations for career change into two main themes. First, we need or desire a change because our career evolved in ways that served our employers (not us). Second, our personal priorities have shifted. Before moving into a deeper look at these two fundamental motivations, there are also a handful of motivations that, after more serious contemplation, lead back to the two fundamental motivations above.

For example, you might have thought, *I want a new challenge.* Or, *I need a change of scenery.* Or, *I need a change of pace.* Mild, moderate, or severe burnout can be motivation for a career transition. Despite your best efforts and intentions otherwise, your career may unfold in a way where there is an actual or a perceived lack of opportunity. Or, the opportunity that is available may not be the opportunity you seek. In these circumstances, a career change is a legitimate path toward new challenges, a change of scenery, a new pace, a reduction in burnout, and better opportunities.

A common motivation for seeking a transition into data science that our friends Dav, Pol, and Jodi all experienced was the desire to acquire new skills. All three of these characters sought to more fully and effectively use their analytical skills, which they acquired in other domains and then used to leverage their transition into data science. Mere interest in applying new skills is a common, and legitimate, reason for seeking a career change.

A new career can be a pragmatic choice that may lead to higher pay, fewer hours, more convenient hours, or more manageable responsibilities. The superficiality of these motivations makes them no less valid.

Reminder: Your family and professional network are inclined to support you, regardless of your motivations. You can find the evidence of this support in the success you have achieved on your way to becoming a mid- or late-career professional. Changing your career will not disappoint your friends, family, and professional network. Worst-case scenario: Your career transition will raise a lot of questions. Best-case scenario: Your career transition will excite, invigorate, and inspire your friends, family, and professional network.

To prepare your friends, family, and existing network for your career transition in a manner that will ensure their support and also excite, invigorate, and inspire them, you will need to do two things. First, be clear about the reasons you seek the transition. And second, be clear in your communication regarding those reasons. Below, I outline two of the most common reasons mid- and late-career professionals may seek a transition from one field into another.

Our Career Evolved in Directions That Served Employers (Not Ourselves)

Some seek a career change because they find that their current path has not allowed them to achieve the goals they had originally set for themselves. For example, Daveed wanted to help students finish high school. Ze saw math as a significant barrier to many students. Ze pursued a career as a math teacher and worked with students who needed additional support in math.

As Daveed's work progressed, zis school saw zim as an effective educator. The school promoted zim through the years. Eventually, ze had less time to spend with students in a classroom or within tutoring programs. As an effective educator, zis work evolved in directions that served the employer's priorities (overall school operations) rather than serving Daveed's priorities (working to help students finish school).

The unfortunate result of Daveed's professional success was that opportunities to serve zis own priorities slowly diminished. This is an example of how or why successful professionals may look to transition their career from one field to another.

Daveed is not alone. Many professionals desire for their work to make the world a better place. Upsettingly, many discover their career does not offer opportunities to be of service to others. As careers progress, work-related obligations slowly reduce the time we have for that direct, supportive, and helpful work that originally motivated us.

Personal Priorities Change Over Time

Our sense of priorities will change over time. This change in priorities means it is natural to reconsider choices we made earlier on in our careers. Therefore, it is a sign of worry when anyone does not, at some point, seriously consider a major career shift. Our first few jobs in our career served the priorities we had at the beginning of our career. As those priorities change, we need to evaluate if our earlier career choices still serve our new priorities.

We make major life decisions at a young age when we are less mature, even though we have not yet fully developed our ability to set and maintain our priorities. We skewed our youthful priorities toward youthful pursuits. As we mature, we grow in our ability to set and maintain long-term, mature priorities.

Simultaneously, life circumstances change as we grow. Young ones are born, or they grow older. Our elders become less independent. Those on whom we depended now need us in return. I consider myself fortunate now to have an opportunity to live and work near where my dad lives. I know that as he ages, he will begin depending on me. This kind of changing life circumstances has influenced my sense of priorities. As I work with clients, it is a common refrain to hear, "I am no longer motivated by the thoughts and ideas that were important to me early in my life." Change is a natural function of life. These changes also influence our priorities.

Responding Appropriately

Broadly speaking, there are two potential outcomes when you tell your friends, family, and professional associations that you plan to transition your career into data science. First, the conversations might go well. Second, the conversations might not go so well. In the first case, you will receive warm and enthusiastic encouragement. In the second case, you will receive cool and skeptical discouragement—or outright resistance. This section provides guidance on how you can respond in each case.

How to Respond When Conversations Go Well

This is good. You have positive feedback. The first thing to do is internalize that feedback. When you hear it, make eye contact and verbally acknowledge the feedback. Say thank you and express gratitude. Repeat that feedback to yourself as soon as you can find a moment to yourself. Another helpful technique is to share that feedback with someone else, such as a friend, a colleague, a member of your family, or a professional career coach. You can also write the feedback down to better remember it in the short term and then better appreciate it in the long term.

When Conversations Do Not Go Well

The premise of this chapter is that on balance, your friends, family, and professional connections will be an asset for you. However, sometimes there will be one or more connections in life who do not share the optimism and enthusiasm that most are likely to share. This is not so good.

The first thing you can do is to take a deep breath and try not to take the feedback personally. It can be difficult, but remember that data science remains widely regarded as a new and burgeoning field. Many people—even well-meaning ones—may not understand what data science is or why you would want to transition into that field.

The second thing you can do is to try understanding this person's feelings and concerns. As discussed above, your ability to respond with empathy is important. In some cases, the person may be trying to protect you from what they perceive as a risky or dangerous decision. In other cases, the person may feel threatened by your career change; they might be worried about how it will affect your relationship with them. Your spouse and child(ren), who depend on you for their own livelihood, may react negatively; they may be fearful that your career transition will backfire and inhibit your ability to fully provide for the entire family. As another example, your parents may have reached retirement, and now they rely on you to some extent. Parents who rely on children who are looking at a career transition, in any measure, might have similar selfish reactions.

Once you have taken a step back and tried to understand where the person is coming from, you can then decide how you want to respond. Usually, it will make sense to engage in further discussion and explanation. Consider sharing this book as a resource for your family. Chapters 1 through 3 of this book might help your friends, family, or professional connections better understand what data science is, why it is an appealing career option, and why mid- and late-career professionals often feel motivated to change careers.

In other cases, however, it may be simply best to thank the person for their feedback and move on. I would never advise that you end a relationship over a onetime cool, sullen, or skeptical expression of discouragement or hesitation. Instead, give the conversation a break. Focus on speaking with others who are more supportive. Later, when it feels right for you, consider re-engaging with anyone who was less than fully enthusiastic about your decision to transition into data science.

In the end, it is always your decision as to how you want to proceed. Having a strong and supportive network of family, friends, and professional colleagues will make your career transition easier. However, even when some people in your life are not initially supportive, you can still respond in a way that will minimize any negative impact and allow you to move forward with confidence.

How the Conversations Might Sound

The following is an imaginary account of how Dav communicated with zis family to prepare them for zis transition into data science. Not all of these conversations went well.

Dav had spent years working within both primary and secondary education before beginning a transition into becoming a data scientist.

Dav's family was reluctant at first to accept this change when Dav proposed it to them. Ze had reasons for wanting a change, and zis parents had their own reasons for their hesitation and reluctance.

From Dav's perspective, the education system had not helped zim in achieving the right goals toward zis passions. In the 1990s, many schools sorted students by tracking them into specific career paths. As Dav's school did not track zim for college, ze was not properly prepared to attend college. Ze ended up learning about opportunities to teach English abroad.

Ze studied and saved to become qualified to teach English as a foreign language. Ze eventually completed a Teaching English as a Foreign Language (TEFL) certification, and ze traveled to teach English in Budapest, Hungary. Dav's parents were unable to support zim financially for zis education and during the time spent teaching abroad.

After this, ze returned to the United States to finish college and then worked in administration for higher education. Later, Dav decided to continue zis pursuits in higher education and went into law school. Six years after law school, ze started and then completed a PhD. Whilst studying in the PhD program, Dav gained experience and skills in a range of disciplines, including data science. These new experiences pushed zim to pursue a career in data science.

Through Dav's multiple career changes, it is understandable that zis parents were less than enthusiastic about zis interest in changing once again to follow an interest in data science.

At first, when Dav told zis parents about this intent to alter Dav's career trajectory once more, they did not react positively. Dav had been excited to announce zis intentions, but the family responded in unexpected ways.

"Again?" zis father asked. "Why do you think this path will be the right one? What if you decide you dislike it and then make a change, yet again, a couple of years down the line?"

"We just want you to have a stable career," zis mother said. "If you had stuck to one thing for as long as you have been jumping around, you could be quite successful already."

Pushing past the upsetting implication that Dav was not already successful, Dav could not believe that zis parents would doubt zim in such a way. Ze did not know why they could not just support zis new venture.

Looking back with an empathetic hindsight, ze can see that the parent's reluctance came from a place of care and generosity, not neglect and selfishness. Zis change in careers would likely bring instability and uncertainty, and Dav's parents only wanted zim to be secure and prosperous—hence the doubt. If Dav had considered their perspective, ze could have avoided some measure of personal disappointment and even a few unnecessary arguments.

Dav could have said, "I know you want the best for me. I can see the potential with data science. I know I can grow in this field. I can put my passion behind this."

"How?" zis father might have asked. "Why can't you do that with the job you have already put so much time into?"

"It is a new and uncertain field for me, I know. I simply have different priorities now, unlike back when I began my professional career. This field did not exist earlier in my career. Not the way it does now. I know this is something I enjoy; I would like to see where it leads me."

"I have studied data science in my PhD, remember?" Dav would continue to explain. "It may be a relatively new field, but it is already thriving. The opportunity I have here, to make the most of a growing industry, is far greater than any I can see myself having in higher education. It also helps that it is something I am passionate about, as I felt I was just going through the motions for my last job."

It would take further conversations with similar approaches to help get both of zis parents on board. To reach success in preparing friends and family, Dav needed to maintain composure. Dav and others in similar positions know more about the field of data science than many families and friends do.

To help prepare friends and family, we are their doorway into understanding the new career option and the reasons for that career change. With care and compassion, the conversation will evolve.

For example, Dav also needed to manage conversations with zis spouse. Having had the tough conversation with zis parents earlier on, it made it easier to talk through the issues with zis spouse.

Going into the subsequent conversations, ze could notice the signs of frustration building whenever it felt like ze was not getting zis point across or when ze thought that she was not listening to what ze had to say. Ze steadied zis breathing, as it would mirror the breathing of a calmer person, and then zis body would instinctively react to bring zis own mood gradually down to that of a calm individual. Ze kept eye contact as she spoke so that it was clear ze was listening, which would help her stay calm, too. Ze avoided fidgeting as they talked, to avoid seeming unsure as ze spoke. To reassure others that ze was certain, ze needed to show that ze felt confident in zis decision.

In the conversations that followed for Dav and zis spouse, ze made sure that she felt heard and sure that what ze was doing was in her best interests. Ze realized that even though ze had made the decision with zimself in mind, ze would need to keep everyone else in mind as well. Few committed family members act out of selfishness. Keeping the rest of the family in mind avoids causing unnecessary upset.

It was easy for Dav to see the positives of zis decision. To help others see the positives, ze even taught them some basics about data science. However, learning about data science is not necessarily what cushioned the news about ze's career transition. While teaching them about data science, Dav's family saw the passion and interest. Seeing firsthand that passion and interest did more for helping others in the family adjust than any of the mere explanations about data science and its lucrative prospects.

The conversation always went best when Dav approached it with thought for the other's perspective. In the end, ze was able to bring around zis loved ones, but it took effort and time. The process of preparing friends and family was not overnight or instantaneous either.

In hindsight, Dav would have liked to avoid the difficult conversations with zis parents shortly after deciding to become a data scientist, but ze was happy for the experience in how to handle those situations for when ze spoke to zis spouse.

***

Here are some mindsets that helped me. Like Dav, I started with gratitude. I communicated to friends, family, and my professional associations that without their support, it would have been difficult for me to achieve the success that I had achieved. I reminded my community how thankful I was for their help as they assisted me in reaching where I was in life. I assured my family that it would have been very difficult for me to build my career without their support.

As a mid- or late-career professional who aspires to change careers, you can and should prepare your friends, family, and your professional associations in the same way.

As you communicate gratitude, you should likewise be very clear on why you are making this transition. Finally, continute to keep clear and open communication with friends, family, and your professional associations. If you can tell your family and friends clearly what it is you want and why you want it, then that will allow them to connect with you and support you during this change.

Chapter Summary

As a mid- or late-career professional, making a major career change will likely have a significant impact on your family and professional relationships and associations. However, when done well, acclimating those who will be affected can also facilitate your transition.

Always start with gratitude by expressing your sincere appreciation for the support and guidance you received.

Others in your life may express concerns or disapproval . Be empathetic toward their concerns or even their disapproval. Try to see where they are coming from while still staying firm with your decision.

There are several reasons for making a major career change. For some, your current career may be moving in an undesirable direction. Others have experienced a change in personal priorities. Experiences with burnout may also be a prominent factor. Sometimes, the opportunity for a better position is reason enough for a career change too. It is important to be clear with yourself and others as to why you are making this change. The sample conversations within this chapter can aid you in anticipating different outcomes, so you may decide how you will respond.

There is a fable about happiness. A teacher gives each of her students a balloon and asks them to write their names on their balloon. After piling all the balloons into the hallway, the teacher says, "Go find your balloon." After a while, very few have located their own balloons. Next, the teacher says to everyone, "Pick a balloon, any balloon." The teacher then says, "Give your balloon to its owner." Within moments, everyone has their balloon.

The traditional interpretation of this fable is that balloons are like happiness. Finding happiness on your own is hard, but when you care about someone else's happiness, this leads you to finding your own happiness as well.

I think the balloons are like jobs too. Finding the right job on your own can be tough. Having help from the community makes finding the right job for you a bit less difficult.

CHAPTER 5

The Resume

This chapter will provide specific guidance related to improving your resume. The next chapter will look at the LinkedIn profile, and then Chapter 7 will cover content ideas and advice for your professional portfolio. Through these three chapters, you will learn how to optimize these important tools for your transition as a mid- or late-career professional into the field of data science.

Take the "rules" in this chapter as guidelines. No collection of books will agree on what is the best option for every drafting and formatting question. I designed these guidelines to help you produce readable documents that will showcase your skills and abilities as a data professional. I optimized these rules for mid- and late-career professionals. When you find a point on which you may disagree, seek input from a trusted advisor. Or ask what Daveed, Poleh, or Jodi would do. The guidelines in this portion of this book will serve as a place to start.

Job Document Strategies to Avoid

Here are strategies that may have worked at one point but will probably fall short for most. The problem is that instead of articulating value, these strategies try to game, trick, or rely on "critical mass" or luck.

Avoid:

- Filling your resume with resume builders just to add length to your resume.
- Spamming recruiters and hiring managers.
- Spending all of your time "networking" for the sake of "networking".
- Rushing to apply for every position without ensuring that it aligns with who you are and what you seek for your career.
- Trying to trick an Applicant Tracking System with white-colored keywords that will look "hidden" as you draft but will reveal themselves after automated document processing.
- Including any information not specifically relevant to the job for which you are applying.

General Guide When Writing about Yourself

Before proceeding to the specifics, there are a few bits of advice that apply to all three job documents, including your resume, LinkedIn (or other social media), and your professional portfolio.

Drop Unnecessary Modifiers in Current and Former Job Titles

Nobody needs or wants to misrepresent the truth, but many individuals are too cautious on this point. You can see the unnecessary caution when job seekers use excessive modifiers. For example, most college and university professors start as assistant professors before advancing to associate professors with tenure, and then later to full professors.

We label the most senior role as just *professor.* Thus, the mistake then is to feel that dropping the word *assistant* or *associate* will be a lie. When your audience is non-academic, and you can also be confident that they will not fully understand the seemingly grand distinctions between assistant and associate professorships. The assistant or associate modifiers will make you look far less accomplished than you are. I advise those who were formerly assistant professors to drop the word assistant from their title on a resume (and LinkedIn) when they apply for jobs with non-academic employers.

There are similar patterns in many other professional settings, including law, accounting, and consulting. If you are in these other fields, my advice is to forgo use of the modifiers

111

"assistant," "associate," or "senior." These modifiers only make sense in hyper-specific contexts, which recruiters and hiring managers may not fully understand. When you are not confident that your audience will understand the true meaning of those modifiers, it is best to simplify. Instead of *associate/assistant consultant*, use *consultant*.

Choices of Perspective

For resumes, portfolios, biographic profiles, and professional portfolios, the choices of perspective are first person or third person. First person is when the writer refers directly to themselves by using *I* or *we*. Third person is when the writer refers to themselves indirectly by using *he, she, zim, they*, or other pronouns.

First person example:

My name is Poleh. I am a data scientist with over 10 years of experience in marketing.

Third person example:

Poleh is a data scientist with over 10 years of experience in marketing.

My advice is to write in first-person perspective. This first-person style is more personal and persuasive than the third-person perspective.

General Resume Formatting

Avoid flashy and fancy (for the sake of flashy and fancy alone). Less is more.

> ➤ Use standard, common, pervasive fonts. These are the fonts that everyone knows and that all computers will recognize. Good choices include: Arial, Calibri, **Verdana**, or **Trebuchet**.
>
> ➤ Choose no more than two font colors. Usually, one color is best.
>
> ➤ Use single space.
>
> ➤ Use the same size of margin on all four sides and on all pages. Mid- and late-career professionals often need more space for their experience, so I recommend using 0.75 inches.
>
> ➤ Keep formatting to a minimum (bold, italics, underline, etc.). When formatting, use the document editor's pre-set styles as shown in Figure 5.1.
>
> ➤ Avoid special features that may improve how your resume looks for a human reader, such as page headers, page footers, boxes, columns, tables, or images.
>> ○ Page headers, page footers, boxes, columns, and tables rarely work well with an Applicant Tracking System (ATS). An ATS may "read" and screen applications based on predictive analytics and other simple keyword matching metrics.

- ○ Some ATS have difficulty parsing information within page headers, page footers, boxes, columns, tables, or images. Consequently, if the ATS cannot read your document because of page headers, page footers, boxes, columns, or tables, your resume will not perform well when viewed by ATS screeners.
- ➤ When listing dates, use the year and month format (e.g., June 2024). Mid- and late-career professionals need not list specific days of the month. Other ATS-friendly options: MM/YY or MM/YYYY (06/24 or 06/2024).
- ➤ Do not include images.
  - ○ Images detract from your message. Images might complicate formatting and confound ATS system features. For the same reason, do not use charts or graphs. Save images, charts, and graphs for your portfolio.
- ➤ For mid- and late-career professionals, a resume may be up to two pages.
  - ○ For companies or positions that expect extensive publication or service histories, more pages may be appropriate. For instance, applying to an academic institution may require a long-form resume called a *curriculum vitae,* or CV for short. A CV often has the first two pages of a resume along with additional subsections listing conference topics, articles, and other activities that a university might find important.

➢ If submitting your resume via email (and you are certain the company does not use an ATS), submit your resume as a PDF. If you are submitting your resume via an Applicant Tracking System, submit your resume as a MS Word document saved in Rich Text Format.

➢ Do not attempt to trick ATS with invisible or white-colored fonts.

  ❍ It may seem clever to improve keyword matching by putting words from the job description into the resume, and then changing the font color to white to make it invisible for most human readers.

  ❍ In theory, an ATS will then see those words and count them in the keyword matching process.

  ❍ However, using invisible fonts can backfire. For example, some ATS may sometimes automatically convert all fonts to a visible color, which will then spoil how your resume looks. Also, there are more effective methods that can boost a resume's keyword match rate.[10]

---

[10] In addition to the Applicant Tracking System (ATS) advice given in this chapter, this book's online bonuses include free access to Dr. Nelson's ATS mini-course online. For more information, see https://coaching.adamrossnelson.com/book_bonuses.

The Seven Sections of a Resume

This section instructs you on how to prepare up to seven main sections. Some sections are optional, while others are not. Include each section in the order listed below.

1. Overall Headings (at the top of the first page)

Use the pre-set title style for your name. Use the pre-set subtitle style for the job title you are seeking. Make sure this matches the position description for which you are applying.

Figure 5.1 shows how the top first page of your resume should look. The paragraph marks show the exact editing choices. Notice how a "shift + return" (Apple) or a "shift + enter" (PC) follows the first two lines of the address and contact information block. That "shift + enter" keystroke strategy saves vertical space.

The large arrows in Figure 5.1 emphasize the importance and utility of using the pre-defined styles within your document editing software (Microsoft, n.d.). Figure 5.1 means to show how you can change the font size, color, and other style choices to the pre-defined settings within the "style pallet" or "style pane." All major word processing software offers equivalent tools. Use them.

Using these pre-defined styles provides major benefits:

- Better collaboration. It is quicker to edit the resume.
- Improved accessibility and inclusivity. Anyone using assistive reading software may be better able to read the document.

- Better ATS performance. Some ATS software may rely on these pre-defined styles to navigate and process your document.

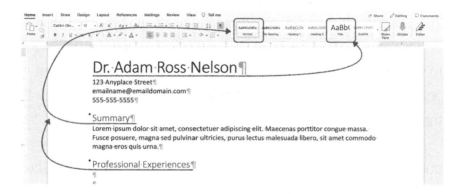

Figure 5.1

Below your name, list contact information.

Include your:

- mailing address
- cell phone number
- professional email address
- GitHub profile (or equivalent) and at least one of your other social media accounts (with content that pertains to the work you will perform if hired)

The reason it is important to include social media references is that as a mid- or late-career professional, you inevitably have some social media history online. By pointing resume readers to a specific social media profile, you can better (although not fully) control what readers will find.

2. The Summary Section

This section is optional. It would use the heading *Summary*. Decide on this based on your research of the position and the company to which you are applying. Each application could be different. If you know a reliable contact at the company, you can ask, "Would they like me to include the summary section on my resume?"

If you are applying to a position that will accept a cover letter, consider putting your summary material in your cover letter. Save the space on your resume for other topics. If you are applying to a position that will not accept a cover letter, this would be an occasion to more strongly consider a summary section on the resume.

A summary section, if you have one, is an opportunity to highlight your strengths and to improve your keyword matching score. If you have a summary section, this is a place in which you have added flexibility that you can use to customize your resume for each specific position. Do not copy and paste the summary from your LinkedIn profile.

Use the following template:

➢ First sentence

In this resume, I summarize my X years of full-time professional experience in [insert the nature of your experience].

➢ Second sentence

My most recent experience includes [insert description of most recent experience].

As applicable, make sure the recent experience speaks to the role you would perform if hired; it must clearly relate to the job description. Do not "beat around the bush."

➢ Third sentence

For example, I used [insert job posting keyword(s)] *to improve/enhance/reduce/increase* [choose something that indicates return on investment] *the organization's* [list a tangible asset or liability].

Make this third sentence as tangible as possible. Give a specific metric if you can. Use it to match keywords in the position description.

➢ Fourth sentence

If you have supervisory or other management experience, include a fourth sentence to describe this:

Throughout my career, I have provided multiple teams with supportive supervision, efficient management of resources, and budgetary oversight.

If applicable, state a specific dollar amount that represents your budgetary management experience.

3. The Education Section

Use the heading *Education*.

If you have a doctorate (PhD, EdD, or equivalent), place the education section immediately following the overall heading (or after the summary section if you have a summary section).

If your highest degree is a master's and you earned it within the previous 6 years, then likewise place your education section immediately following the overall heading (or after the summary section if you have a summary section).

If the time you have spent in school exceeds the time you have spent working full time, you should also place your education section immediately following the overall heading or after the summary section.

Otherwise, place the education section after your professional experiences section but before your publications section.

4. A Section on Toolsets, Software, Languages, Frameworks, etc.

This section is optional. I encourage candidates to speak about toolsets, software, languages, and frameworks in the descriptions associated with each position, rather than listing them in their own section.

The advantage to listing these items along with the jobs in which you utilized the toolset, software, language, or framework is that it provides a more explicit look at the breadth and depth of your experience.

5. The Professional Experiences Section

Use the heading *Professional Experiences*.

If you are certain that an ATS will not presort your resume, it may be appropriate to sort positions by function. We call this a *functional resume*.

However, if it is possible that an ATS will presort your resume, a *chronological resume* is the better choice. When using chronological organization, be sure your two most recent positions appear on the first page.

List titles that match keywords in the position description. Speak with your references to ensure they will verify these titles. Make sure your titles match your LinkedIn profile.

6. A Publications Section

Some employers will expect a publication history for certain positions. Information about this expectation is part of what you should learn about in your background research. If the employer does not expect or require this section, consider it optional.

Include this section (even if it is optional) if you have publications that meet the criteria listed below:

- You have two or three publications that are closely related to the work you will perform if hired. (Never list publications that are not related to the work you would perform if hired.)
- The most recent example was disseminated less than 8 years ago.

In the special case where you have only one publication, do not list it on your resume. Instead, save that publication as something you can share with the recruiter or hiring manager once you speak with them. You can also treat or highlight single, one-off publications as a part of your portfolio. If you submit a cover letter, mention a single publication there.

If you have over three publications, select a mix of publications that are most relevant, that will improve your keyword match rate, and that were distributed in the most prestigious venues— peer-reviewed journals, books, academic conferences, national print media, or well-known blogs. Publications in a resume can improve your ATS keyword match rate when the publication titles have keywords that match the position description.

If you wish to list blog posts (such as articles on LinkedIn, Medium, or your own platform), there are at least two options.

If you are a frequent contributor to one online publication or platform (e.g. Medium's *Towards Data Science*, *Towards AI*, *Hacker Noon*, *KDnuggets*, or *Open Data Science*), it usually works best to list two or three individual articles that are most related to the work you will perform if hired. Select article titles that will improve your keyword match rate.

If you are a frequent contributor to multiple online publications or platforms, instead of listing individual articles, list an index page with links to individual articles. For example, if you have articles at https://medium.com, you can list your main profile URL, such as: https://adamrossnelson.medium.com.

7. A References Section

Listing professional references is optional. If the job application's instructions ask for this on your resume, be sure to include it. If you do list references, list up to three references (unless specifically instructed otherwise).

Chapter Summary

As a mid- or late-career professional, you have worked hard to get to where you are, so do not downplay previous experience. On your resume, be proud and showcase all that you can bring to the potential position.

This chapter covered tips on resume strategies to avoid, guidelines for writing about yourself on a resume or other job document, and resume formatting guidance. This chapter also included helpful advice in preparing a resume that will perform well in automated ATS scoring systems.[11]

---

[11] Reminder: In addition to the Applicant Tracking System (ATS) advice given in this chapter, this book's online bonuses include 30 days of free access to Dr. Nelson's ATS mini-course online. For more information, see https://coaching.adamrossnelson.com/book_bonuses.

There are seven sections to a data professional's resume: headings, summary, education, professional experience, publications, references, and an optional separate section on toolsets/software/languages/frameworks. Refer back to this chapter for instructions on how to best fill out each section.

Once you finish tailoring your resume for a data science position, you will be ready to use its information and follow the steps in Chapter 6 to build your LinkedIn profile.

CHAPTER 6

The LinkedIn Profile

You want your LinkedIn to speak to one group: your future supervisor, co-workers, and their recruiters. The singular focus of this chapter is to help you update your LinkedIn profile. Importantly, this chapter will provide advice beyond what you should say and how you should say it. For example, you will receive detailed advice on the settings you can update or adjust in order to optimize your LinkedIn profile for the purposes of supporting your transition into data science.

LinkedIn is the world's largest professional network with over 830 million members in over 200 countries worldwide. Prospective employers will review your profile on this site. Recruiters will use LinkedIn to find candidates like you. When you plan it out correctly, LinkedIn is also a good place to host professional portfolio entries; making LinkedIn an aspect of your portfolio strategy gives you a reason to send recruiters, hiring managers, and prospective co-workers to this platform to learn more about you.

The mission of LinkedIn is simple: connect the world's professionals to make them more productive and successful. LinkedIn does this by supporting your ability to write and publish posts, status updates, polls, discussions, articles, and documents, as well as engage in other activities. Your activity displays on your profile's activity section and shares with your connections and followers in their news feeds and sometimes through their notifications.

On LinkedIn, your portfolio entries can be in the form of simple posts (also known as a status update). You also have the option of using any of LinkedIn's many other formats. As a professional, and as a job candidate, having a place to host items that showcase your work and skills is an asset. LinkedIn is the place for this.

Any information you place on LinkedIn to showcase your work constitutes a professional portfolio entry. For example, among data scientists, it is popular to make a Jupyter notebook into a PDF and then post that PDF as a document carousel on LinkedIn. Another option is to write articles on the platform. A LinkedIn article resembles a blog post.

The next chapter elaborates more on strategies related to building a distributed professional portfolio. Before you can leverage LinkedIn as a place to distribute your portfolio entries, it is important to give LinkedIn a polish. This chapter will help you accomplish that polish.

The Most Common Mistake Is the Easiest to Fix

I, and others, sometimes ask on social media a version of the question, "Is your profile up to date?" On LinkedIn, the response is usually in the neighborhood of 40% saying no and 60% saying yes. Multiple websites report similar statistics. An out-of-date profile is one of the most common mistakes many will make online. Further, it is one of the easiest mistakes to remedy.

Some of the easiest career advice to give is that you should attend job interviews in professional attire. It would be a red flag if anyone, anywhere, attended a job interview wearing underclothing. Keeping the default settings on your LinkedIn or other social media is the online equivalent to running around town undressed.

Likewise, outside the context of a career search, it would be unwise to attend a business lunch in older or outdated clothing. The clothing analogy illustrates the importance of optimizing your LinkedIn in a manner that will present your best self as an ideal candidate for the positions you seek in your career.

You should align every aspect of your profile and your activity with your desired role. This means forgoing opportunities related to sharing, posting, or commenting on anything that does not align with your desired role. You will not need to click aimlessly through LinkedIn and its settings; this section will guide you through making a base set of updates that will bring your profile up to date. If you follow this set of rules, you will prepare a LinkedIn profile that shows you are a serious professional who is capable and credible in your desired role.

Why Data Professionals Need a Strong LinkedIn

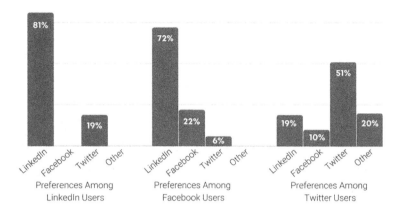

Figure 5.2

Across LinkedIn and Facebook, data science users report preferring LinkedIn as the place to go when looking for others in the field whom they know, like, and trust. Even among Twitter users, LinkedIn is the second most preferred platform.

Some of these rules may require you to change your social media philosophy. For example, some may use LinkedIn as a social network for connecting with friends, co-workers, and former co-workers. Some may use LinkedIn to connect with civic associates at churches or volunteer organizations.

To follow the advice of this chapter means to approach LinkedIn specifically as a job search tool—nothing else. Thus, I repeat from earlier: You want your LinkedIn to speak to one group: your future supervisor, co-workers, and their recruiters.

If you approach LinkedIn with this focus in mind, it will speak for you whenever you are not available to speak for yourself. LinkedIn is your personal billboard. Your LinkedIn's sole purpose is to sell you as a data scientist.

Claim a Custom URL

If you have not already done so, customize your uniform resource locator (URL). Do this on LinkedIn by clicking on *Edit public profile & URL*. Then click, *Edit your custom URL*. Choose a URL that will be easy for you and others to remember. Less is more. No need to be fancy.

Preparing a custom URL communicates that you care about being easily found and recognized. From a tech organization's perspective, it shows that you care about the user experience. By claiming and sharing your custom URL, you show that you have thought through reducing the challenges others might face in finding information about you online. By extension, it shows that you can think through the user experience for the products and services associated with your prospective employer's customers and clients.

The Heading Content

The heading content (the top portions and sections of your profile) is where you can ensure that your goals and purposes for the platform are clear. Below are instructions on how to access the edit features. First, take a moment to think about what you will say regarding your goals and purposes.

> For example, you might say something like this in your about section:

> *I am a data scientist with an extensive background in marketing. After over 15 years of professional experience in marketing, and advanced marketing analytics, I have transitioned into data science.*

> A professional with more experience in data science might write:

> *With over 15 years of professional experience in marketing and data science, I have transitioned my career through advanced marketing analytics and then into data science.*

When visiting your profile, your heading content will usually be the first thing anyone sees. Before even visiting your profile, many will see some of this heading content because this portion of your portfolio will populate search results and page previews.

To edit this information, click the pencil/edit icon in the upper right portion of the section at the top of your profile. It will be to the far right of your name.

- Make sure you display your full and real name (the name by which everyone knows you).
- Avoid generalizations. Be specific. If your current job title matches your desired job title, list your current job title. If your desired job title does not match your current title, list your desired job title—but only if your skills, abilities, and experiences justify claiming the desired job title. Earlier sections in this book discussed how to determine if your skills, abilities, and experiences justify claiming your desired job title.
- Since this field will be searchable by recruiters, list job-specific keywords. For example, you might attach after your job title, "UX Research & Data Science—Natural language processing & data visualization."
- There is a place to specify your current position. Make sure this matches your current position. If you are currently unemployed, list your most recent position.
- List the country and region in which you wish to work. If you are currently moving, or planning to move soon, list the country or region in which you plan to work. Even for remote work, and even since the Covid-19 pandemic, country and region remain important search parameters for many recruiters or hiring managers.
- List the most populated geographic center of your region.
  - For example, instead of Oak Park, IL, put Chicago, IL. Or instead of Silver Spring, MD, put

Washington, DC. Instead of Garland, TX, put Dallas, TX. Instead of Tigard, OR, put Portland, OR.

○ If you are planning a move (and you know where to), list your future location. Look up and use a postal code that matches the location you listed.

LinkedIn makes you choose one industry. A problem with this option is that the options in this list of industries seem to conflate industry, role, and profession. Notably, data science is not on this industry list. Data science or data scientist is the role, yet data scientists work in many industries. To transition into or level up as a data professional, it is important to change industries periodically.

Thus, there are two options here:

1. If you have domain knowledge and domain experience in an industry in which you wish to continue working, list that industry. For example, Daveed worked for many years in higher education. During zis data science job search, ze continued listing higher education as zis industry. Pol listed health care for her industry.

2. If you are open to working in any industry, choose one that most closely represents your background while relating to the broadest range of career possibilities.

Background Banner Photo

Do not rely on LinkedIn's generic background photos. The first and best option for a background photo is one that shows you doing work. For example, giving a presentation at work is a good option.

Other options:

- A photo of your current workplace
  - An example of this would be you with smiling co-workers standing around corporate signage (interior or exterior). Or you solo next to corporate signage. Or just the signage works well too.
- A photo of you engaging in professional development
  - For example, you and fellow professionals at a professional conference.
- Stock imagery (that you use with permission, such as from Unsplash.com)
- Original artwork
  - You can use Fiverr, Upwork, or another online marketplace to hire an artist who will prepare a background for you.
  - Avoid skimping on this. If you have the resources to hire an artist who can prepare for you a banner photo for a few dozen dollars (U.S.), then consider the option. This small

investment made for the sake of a lucrative
and rewarding career will provide a return.
- A design of your own making
  - ○ Many design platforms have simplified the
    process of designing a personal banner for
    LinkedIn, or other social platforms. Consider
    using Canva.com for this.

Here are examples that may work well as sources of
inspiration. For access to these documents as templates in
Canva and PowerPoint, grab this book's bonus package at
https://coaching.adamrossnelson.com/book_bonuses.

Profile Portrait Photo

Make sure you have a portrait photo. Conventional wisdom is that LinkedIn's recommendations and algorithms favor profiles with photos.

Here are some guidelines for your photo:

- Use a photo of yourself.
- Make sure you are smiling.
- Make it a portrait (headshot). Do not use a full body photo.
- Consider getting a professional portrait.
- If you elect not to get a professional portrait, have someone take your photo for you. Choose

an overcast or partly cloudy day, so there will be diffused lighting. Find a place to stand with an attractive wooded background for the photo.
- Have a fresh and contemporary haircut or style.
- Be in professional attire.
  - Note that "professional" is a social construct that can work to reinforce bias and prejudice related to race, gender, ability, social class, etc.
  - Accordingly, explore what "professional" means to you plus what "professional" means to the organizations you wish to join. Decide on your attire based on what you discover through that exploration.
- Consider using photofeeler.com. Some career service professionals will offer clients access to their Photofeeler accounts for no charge.

The About Section

Use this space. To their detriment, some leave this space blank. Do not miss the opportunity to tell your story. The about space on LinkedIn is an opportunity to improve how your profile may perform in search results.

- Take advantage of the online format, as it does not restrict you in the same way an old-fashioned paper resume restricts you. No page limits here!

- Make sure this section includes keywords associated with your desired professional roles.
- Use this space to highlight your accomplishments. Do not be shy about showing your professional accomplishments.
- Avoid writing about what you "hope to do" or the kinds of jobs you "hope to find" in the about section (or anyplace on your LinkedIn profile). As a mid- or late-career professional, your career goals have moved beyond *hope*—you are a bona fide, highly accomplished professional.
- I recommend writing in first-person perspective. This means writing "I am . . ." and "I have . . ." instead of "Ada is . . .", "Pol works for . . .", or "Daveed produces . . ."
- If you have extensive public-facing work products (white papers, publications, presentations, videos, etc.), the about section is where you can provide links for these. Keep in mind that these links will not be clickable.

The Featured Section and Your Activity

These two sections are the easiest to let fall out of date. There are two strategies that can prevent these two sections from growing stale. The first is to focus on content and activity that will be timeless. Marketers call this timeless content *evergreen*.

The second strategy is to groom these sections often. I recommend that job seekers use both strategies.

The featured section allows four types of content: posts, articles, links, and media. There is nothing wrong with having your featured section be only four posts. Nothing fancy is necessary.

Some great content you can find in a featured section are links to:

- Corporate web pages that offer additional information about the profile owner
- Cheat sheet style presentations that cover an important technical or coding topic
- An updated resume (use PDF format)
- A PDF of a Jupyter notebook that demonstrates one or more machine learning techniques
- GitHub repositories
- Medium articles

Generally, the activity section will show your most recent activities. This is a reminder to make sure everything you do on LinkedIn aligns with your desired role. Make sure the topics you discuss directly relate to your work and desired role.

Additional guidelines:

- Avoid negative activity.
- Avoid spelling errors.
- When posting, use hashtags.
  - Three (or about that many) hashtags will keep your posts professional while boosting engagement and exposure.
- The best time to post is in the morning (when your audience arrives at work), at lunch (when your audience might have a breather to browse online), and late in the workday (not late at night).

The Experience Section

LinkedIn sorts each experience and position into chronological order. Take full advantage of the recently expanded fields that are available for each of your positions in the experience section. For example, there are at least seven employment types: full-time, part-time, volunteer, internship, special employment programs, probationary, and contract.

Here is each item you will fill out when adding a new experience:

- ➤ Title

  Use titles that you have on your resume and that your references will verify.

- ➤ Employment type

  This one is relatively new. It lets you specify the type of employment. When you have multiple types of employment at the same organization, this will enrich how your experiences appear. For some locations, there are location-specific employment types.

- ➤ Company

  Ideally, each company you list on your profile will have a logo. If one of your companies does not have a logo, it may be because they have not formed a LinkedIn page or because they have not added a logo to their page. In these cases, you can contact the company to encourage them to add a logo or form a page on LinkedIn. If you own the company or organization, make a page on LinkedIn that you can then associate with your profile. Creating a page for the company will let you and others associated with the company have that logo on their profile.

➢ Start date / end date

Make sure these match your resume.

➢ Description

Use this as an opportunity to describe the work you did. Describe why your work mattered. Identify your accomplishments in specific and tangible terms (exact figures if possible).

Keep word counts roughly equal among the descriptions for each position. Having one section with 1,000 words while others only have 100 words will make it look as though you were not well-accomplished across all roles, or that you do not equally value all of your work.

Education

Complete an education section for all of your college degrees. The name of the school(s), degree(s), field(s) of study, and years should all match what you listed on your resume. Most candidates based in the United States can leave the grade field blank. The activities and societies sections are often best presented as a bulleted list.

Volunteer Experience

List any and all of your volunteer experiences that are related to the role(s) to which you aspire. List the organization, the cause, your role, and the start and end dates.

If the organization's name or your role is directly related to the roles to which you aspire, you can leave the description blank. If that organization or your role is not related to the roles to which you aspire, use the description section to make that connection.

Skills and Endorsements

This is another section that requires active grooming. Grooming this section means checking the settings so that the skills you want endorsed will appear in order for others to endorse you.

Choose the skills most connected to and valued in your desired role, and then consider asking trusted colleagues to endorse you in these skills.

LinkedIn has a *skill quiz*, which will help you prepare this section. If you feel the skill quiz will improve your presentation in this section, use it.

If you are looking for data science or data analytics, the following is a list of endorsements you may look to seek (if they are justified): C/C++, Python, TensorFlow, R, SAS, SPSS, Stata, SQL, Keras, Tableau, AWS, MATLAB, Hadoop, and Spark. Depending on your experiences, others may be more appropriate. Enter skill endorsements for others you know. Be generous but also be genuine.

Recommendations

LinkedIn lets you ask a recommender for revision. Consider asking for revisions on recommendations that may be out of date. Coach those that send recommendations your way on which keywords to use. They can help you if they are related to the work that you aspire to perform.

You can turn the visibility of individual recommendations on or off. Work to make sure your profile shows the recommendations that are most complimentary. The best recommendations are from your co-workers and supervisors as they can speak to your skills and accomplishments. After that, recommendations that speak to your work ethic are also beneficial. This information can verify and validate the claims made in other portions of your profile.

Accomplishments

This section is optional. It is usually better to list accomplishments in the descriptions of your work, education, or volunteer experience, wherever is most applicable.

When an accomplishment is a project or a publication, consider including it in the featured section (discussed above). The featured section gets more traffic and attention from those that visit your profile.

Interests

Most of our interests are broader than our careers. When you like or follow a page on LinkedIn, it will appear as one of your interests. It is okay to have interests appear here that are above and beyond your career—mostly because it is difficult to avoid. However, make sure that at least some of these interests relate to your career goals and aspirations.

Your Profile Settings

Under the profile *jobs* section, click on *application settings*. Here you can upload a resume. If you do, make sure you upload your resume and that it is up to date.

The other settings in this section, if enabled, make it easier for you to use LinkedIn when applying for jobs:

- Under *setting & privacy*, click on *data privacy*. Enable the option to *Share your profile when you click Apply for a job*.

- Update your commute preference in a manner that is consistent with your preferences.
- For maximum exposure, enable the setting that signals your interest to recruiters and companies for which you have created job alerts.
- Under *visibility*, change your settings to be as visible as you are comfortable doing. Remember that during a job search, you can increase your visibility temporarily and then later reduce it once you find a position.

Job Alerts

According to LinkedIn's documentation, "You can create job alerts on LinkedIn to stay updated with new job postings that match your preferences. You can choose whether you want to receive these alerts on a daily or weekly basis through email, app notifications, or both." Use these resources and make full use of this function.

Chapter Summary

With many employers, the job applicant review process will go deeper than the resume and past work experiences. Employers may also research candidates on social media sites. Before you cringe, remember that managing what employers find about you on social media can work to your advantage. Data science users report preferring LinkedIn as the place to go when looking for others in the field whom they know, like, and trust. A polished LinkedIn profile will support you in confidently presenting yourself to your prospective employers.

This chapter guided you step by step through each section of the LinkedIn profile: heading content, background banner photo, profile photo, about, featured, experience, education, volunteer work, skills, recommendations, accomplishments, interests, profile settings, and job alerts.

This chapter provided advice that went above and beyond what to say and how to say it by moving you through the LinkedIn platform, section-by-section and setting-by-setting. Closely following this chapter's advice will improve your experience on the platform.

If followed, the set of guidelines presented will help you prepare a LinkedIn profile that shows you are a serious professional who is capable and credible in your desired role. You should align every aspect of your profile and your activity with your desired role. The strictest adherent to this advice would be to forgo opportunities to share, post, or comment on anything that is unrelated.

In the best-case scenario, recruiters will find you because you updated your LinkedIn settings and kept your LinkedIn profile active. When done well, this means recruiters may begin contacting and recruiting you.

Remember, you deserve a seat at the table. You have taken the time and energy needed to prepare yourself for this next career step—to become a data scientist—and you are more ready than you know!

## CHAPTER 7

The Distributed Portfolio Strategy

My sincerest goal for you as you read this chapter is that you see building and maintaining a professional portfolio should not be a burden. The practical advice I give in this chapter involves using your existing work as portfolio entries. Here, you will find specific information on a variety of platforms that can host entries in your distributed professional data science portfolio, with an emphasis on making your GitHub recruiter ready. This chapter also features 10 specific ideas that will inspire you as you look to produce and create new entries for your portfolio.

The avant-garde among those who peddle career advice sometimes say, "A personal brand is the new portfolio." As a place to start thinking about your portfolio, this advice is not wrong. To elaborate on this advice and to make this advice more actionable, I suggest to anyone interested in building a professional portfolio to pursue a distributed portfolio strategy. Much in the same way marketing professionals design a corporate brand to remind customers about a product and service, a distributed portfolio can remind prospective employers, recruiters, hiring managers, and co-workers who you are and how good you are at data science.

Individuals do not need the same kind of branding that corporations or consumer goods need. Instead, the most effective strategy here is to establish a strong persona as a professional data scientist, which will remind folks about yourself over time.

A distributed portfolio strategy involves producing and sharing portfolio entries across a range of platforms. By distributing your portfolio, you increase its visibility among those in the data science field and those who can help you enter or level up in the field. In my data science career, I was fortunate enough to receive a job offer (twice) from a prominent data science organization. Those offers were directly motivated by, at least in part, my portfolio and its distributed strategy. I ended up not accepting those offers. The purpose of this story is to illustrate the utility of my distributed portfolio approach.

A data science organization reached out to me because of entries in my distributed data science portfolio. If inquiries from data science recruiters is not in itself justification to support the importance of a data science portfolio, well, the story gets better. During technical interviews, I pointed to entries in my distributed data science portfolio (all available online) that related to what we were discussing in the technical interview.

In one case, the hiring manager was preparing me for an upcoming technical interview. The hiring manager said, "Bring a project to the technical interview that you have worked on and be prepared to talk about it." For me, with my distributed data science portfolio, bringing a project to the technical interview was as easy as bringing four web links (URLs): one to an article I wrote that outlined the project, another to a related article I wrote that supported the project, a third to a GitHub repository, and a fourth to a YouTube video that also explained the project.

The remainder of this chapter will outline a range of platforms frequented by data scientists on which you might place entries in a distributed professional portfolio. This section will outline specific ideas that may inspire you as you look to create content for your portfolio. And lastly, this chapter will offer an in-depth look at how you can establish and configure a profile on GitHub, which will serve as a centralized back end for the rest of your portfolio entries on other platforms.

Portfolio Platforms

While introducing readers to each of these platforms, this section summarizes how each platform may support data science portfolio entries. For example, Medium.com hosts content primarily in a format that resembles online magazine articles or blog posts. However, GitHub hosts content primarily within virtual containers called *repositories*. Each repository can contain code, Jupyter notebooks, documentation, images, and other project-related documentation.

The main recommendation of this chapter is that readers pursue a strategy that involves producing and placing portfolio entries via multiple platforms. When done well, this strategy creates a cumulative effect, where the value of all components is greater than the raw sum of each individual component.

GitHub

I start the list of options with GitHub because it is a niche site specifically made for software professionals. However, the data science community has extensively adopted GitHub. After sharing more about GitHub, and other platforms, this chapter later provides an extensive point-by-point, section-by-section, setting-by-setting guide on how to optimize your GitHub as a job candidate in data science.

GitHub's slogan is "Where the world builds software." GitHub is a useful place to share data science content, such as data science portfolio entries. Because its platform emphasizes experimentation and collaboration, the platform also makes the information it hosts discoverable and highly shareable.

GitHub's user experience permits users to establish a public profile page that highlights up to six *pinned* projects. Each project on GitHub is known as a *repository*. Each repository can host a specific data science portfolio entry.

Medium

This platform shares the following on its about page:

> The best ideas can change who we are. Medium is where those ideas take shape, take off, and spark powerful conversations. We're an open platform where over 100 million readers come to find insightful and dynamic thinking. Here, expert and undiscovered voices alike dive into the heart of any topic and bring new ideas to the surface. Our purpose is to spread these ideas and deepen understanding of the world.

As a place to position distributed portfolio entries, the main format Medium supports is articles that resemble online magazine articles or blog posts. This format is perfect for data scientists. You can share your own experiences and advice, and you can educate people on data science in an engaging way.

You will not only be helping others. Writing on Medium can motivate others to reach out and help you, too. Thus, you will also learn from some of the best minds in the industry. Medium has a powerful community that is usually happy to provide feedback and help you grow as a writer.

Medium contains at least 1.4 million pages that reference *data science*. Importantly, the Medium platform supports some of the largest online publications devoted to the topics of data science, artificial intelligence, machine learning, and statistics.

An advantage of using Medium is that you can earn money when others read your stories. And, if you submit your work to Medium publications, you will extend the reach of your portfolio's distribution. If you are new to Medium and decide to join as a paid reader, consider using my referral link: https://adamrossnelson.medium.com/membership

Quora

This platform pursues the following mission:

> Quora's mission is to share and grow the world's knowledge. Not all knowledge can be written down, but much of that which can be, still isn't. It remains in people's heads or only accessible if you know the right people. We want to connect the people who have knowledge to the people who need it, to bring together people with different perspectives so they can understand each other better, and to empower everyone to share their knowledge for the benefit of the rest of the world.

The purpose of Quora is to ask questions and get answers from experts. It is a great way to learn about new topics, get expert opinions on important issues, and connect with other professionals. Shortly before this book's publication, Google returned 1.5 million search results for the search: site:www.quora.com "data science." Another similar site that structures itself around discussion or question and answer is Reddit.

Personal Websites

The purpose of a personal website can be much more open-ended than sites like GitHub, Medium, Quora, and others. Websites offer you the widest array of format options for professional portfolio entries. On your own website, you have more control; a personal website allows you to control the narrative around your work and present yourself in the best light possible.

Building a website for your portfolio should not be expensive, nor should it be complicated. However, a website should not be the start and end of your portfolio. Remember to take advantage of the distributed approach. Use a website in concert with other platforms.

If you decide to build a website, consider https://carrd.co. Not only is a Carrd website easy to make, it offers a rich feature set on their free tier. They also offer paid enhancements. However, for a data professional on the job search, the free version is easily more than sufficient. Consider using my referral code: https://try.carrd.co/arn2020

Other Options

You can place distributed portfolio entries on any of the remainder of these platforms listed here. In a sense, anything Google will return when someone searches your name (or your email address) is a component of your distributed portfolio entry. Make sure your activity on these other platforms reflects well upon you as a professional.

These other platforms include the Stack Exchange network of websites. Other important places to consider placing and polishing your information would be YouTube, Twitter, Pinterest, Instagram, and TikTok. As you review these other platforms, you might be tempted to think, *I am not very active there*, and then proceed to ignore it. Before you dismiss this advice, at the very minimum, review and polish your information on these sites. Ensure that the information is at least up-to-date. Perhaps consider adding additional information that will work as a portfolio entry. Keep in mind that as a mid- or late-career professional, you may have made comments, posts, videos, or photos years ago that you have long since forgotten. Therefore, it may be worthwhile to find and then remove any unfavorable or unflattering information.

Overall Platform Advice

Some additional guidance that applies equally to all of the above platforms:

- Keep it simple.

  If you have never built a website before, then use a template. Playing around with how different elements line up on a web page is frustrating and can result in a website that looks unprofessional.

- Take inspiration from others.

  Look at other GitHub repositories, Medium articles, Quora posts, and websites. Note what you like and do not like about each site. Pick others that you admire, and then emulate their work.

- Get input.

  Ask for feedback from anyone whose opinion you trust. But remember: The most valuable feedback will be from those who might hire you (or who have recently hired data scientists).

- Proofread.

  Use an automated writing assistant such as Grammarly, ProWritingAid, or Hemingway Editor. I am a fan of ProWritingAid, whose desktop editor works well with Markdown (a common online document markup syntax).[12]

- Consider hiring help.

  Often the word count for your portfolio entries (such as blogs or repository ReadMe.md files) will be low. Therefore, the cost of hiring an editor will also be low. Proper grammar and spelling conveys professionalism.

---

[12] Consider using these referral links if you choose to further explore ProWritingAid: https://prowritingaid.com/grammar-checker?rafid=gKBaK (a grammar checker) or https://prowritingaid.com/en/App/Features?afid=27636 (an updated list of features).

Content Ideas for Your Portfolio

In this subsection, I write about 10 portfolio content ideas. You can copy them. Use them as templates to showcase your unique thoughts, ideas, skills, experiences, and abilities.

Data Sets That Load in a Single Line of Code

This example is based on an article I wrote for *Towards Data Science* (Nelson, 2022b). It was fun to write. It was hard to write, too. Find a number of data sets on your own that are out in the wild. Write code that will load that data in Python, R, or another platform with only a single line of code. Write an article about it that showcases the code. This will be useful for readers who need quick data for training, testing, education, and demonstration purposes.

Find data related to your own hobbies and interests. If you are a college sports enthusiast, consider another title: *22 College Sports Data Sets That Load in a Single Line of Code.* Do not get hung up on the number—go long if you can and are inspired to do so. Or go shorter if that is more your speed. Have fun with this one.

Data Collection

Collecting data is a serious job in data science as well as being one of our toughest jobs. This portfolio entry idea involves the use of two to three platforms. First, you will collect data (from online, real life, your own survey, etc.). It does not matter where you collect the data from as long as the data will be interesting to someone (and you have permission to both use and redistribute that data).

Second, you will write about how you collected the data. If you used Google Forms, for example, you can also write about that platform's strengths and weaknesses as you encountered them. You will then write about how you prepared the data for analysis and distribution to others for their analysis. The article you write will go online, and it will include code snippets, screen capture illustrations, and possibly screen recording video of you doing this work. You may write multiple articles about your data collection and preparation processes.

Lastly, you will post the code, supporting documentation (the documentation is really important), and the data via GitHub.

Exploratory Data Analysis (Data Visualization)

Similar to the previous option of collecting data as a portfolio entry, it is a common tactic to take an existing data set and conduct exploratory data analysis. If you need data to work with for this, see my article I mentioned above: *93 Data Sets That Load in a Single Line of Code*. Or better yet, use data from your article: *22 College Sports Data Sets That Load in a Single Line of Code*. Another good option would be to write an article that focuses on any data you specifically collected yourself (see the previous suggestion). By referencing your own work, the distributed portfolio builds on itself.

Compete in a Competition

Another option is to participate in an online competition. For example, Maven Analytics (https://www.mavenanalytics.io)

offers regular competitions related to data exploration and data visuals. Their topics are fun and interesting. The popular site Kaggle (https://www.kaggle.com) also provides access to online competitions. Maven and Kaggle usually find, prepare (at least somewhat), and provide (at least in part) the data for you.

A non-exhaustive list of additional platforms that routinely offer online competitions: Driven Data (https://www.drivendata.org), Omdena (https://omdena.com), Data Camp (https://www.datacamp.com), and Analytics Vidhya (https://datahack.analyticsvidhya.com).

Winning a competition like this can give a nice boost to your know/like/trust factor from the notoriety associated with winner announcements.

Sentiment Analysis

The top three cloud platform providers give step-by-step tutorials on how to build a sentiment analysis project using their products and services. If you spend the time working through one (or all) of these tutorials, you can create portfolio entries from your notes, screen captures, and results.

This activity will give you fodder for multiple articles. If planned and implemented well, you have the opportunity to organize it all into an impressive GitHub repository. A larger-scale GitHub repository that supports this kind of distributed portfolio entry will be impressive because it will show your ability to plan, document, and maintain a complex project.

You can find these tutorials here:

- Google (using Google Cloud Natural Language API): https://cloud.google.com/natural-language/docs/sentiment-tutorial
- AWS (using Amazon Comprehend): https://aws.amazon.com/getting-started/hands-on/analyze-sentiment-comprehend
- Azure (using Azure Synapse): https://learn.microsoft.com/en-us/azure/synapse-analytics/machine-learning/tutorial-cognitive-services-sentiment

These tutorials are designed to let you quickly start exploring and developing these applications. Even if you have little programming knowledge, most of the tutorials should be accessible to you.

Beginner-Friendly Data Science Tools Accepting Contributions

The process of finding an open-source tool that is accepting contributions, searching for a contribution you can make, and then implementing that contribution is one that also makes for an impressive distributed portfolio entry. For example, data scientists are likely familiar with the open-source project called Pandas. The authors of Pandas explain, on GitHub, "All contributions, bug reports, bug fixes, documentation improvements, enhancements, and ideas are welcome."

There are at least three smart reasons to make contributions to open-source software projects:

1. Pure altruism, meaning you can make the world a better place for others (in general, and more specifically in the field of data science).
2. Contributing to open-source projects and tools will help you learn.
3. Making contributions to open-source projects is a good way to expand your professional portfolio.

Other than Pandas, there are many other well-known, open-source data science projects that are receptive toward contributions by newer data science professionals. Here I discuss two options. After Pandas, the second to look at is sklearn or scikit-learn.

Sklearn is a good place for newer professionals to start because as its contribution guide explains:

> *This project is a community effort, and everyone is welcome to contribute . . . We are a community based on openness and friendly, didactic discussions. We aspire to treat everybody equally, and value their contributions. We are particularly seeking people from underrepresented backgrounds in Open-Source Software and scikit-learn in particular to participate and contribute*

their expertise and experience. Decisions are made based on technical merit and consensus.

Another place to contribute your work that is worth considering is a package called ydata-profiling (until recently known as *pandas-profiling*). To guide users in making contributions, ydata-profiling breaks out potential contributions into five categories: exploratory data analysis, stability (which includes performance and restricted environment compatibility), interaction and user experience, community, and machine learning (Nelson, 2021 and 2022d).

Make a Rosetta Stone

The original Rosetta Stone was an actual stone. The stone was "inscribed with three versions of a decree issued . . . on behalf of King Ptolemy V Epiphanes. The top and middle texts are in Ancient Egyptian using hieroglyphic and Demotic scripts respectively, while the bottom is in Ancient Greek. The decree has only minor differences between the three versions, making the Rosetta Stone key to deciphering Egyptian scripts." (Wikipedia, 2022e)

Thus, for programmers, data scientists, and other technical professionals, a Rosetta Stone is a crosswalk that shows us how to execute similar functions in multiple programming languages side-by-side. Here is an example, shown in Figure 7.1 is a high-level example outline of how you could structure Rosetta Stone.

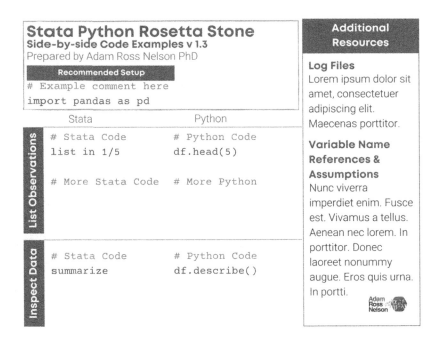

Figure 7.1

The first way to make a Rosetta Stone is to create a document or a website that shows general code examples, in different languages, side by side. The above example in Figure 7.1 shows general code examples in two different languages side by side. I abbreviated and included "lorem ipsum" text in the example here to help make sure it is readable on the pages of this book. For other examples see https://coaching. adamrossnelson.com/book_bonuses.

A second way to make a Rosetta Stone is to port a project from one language to another. If you have a project that you executed in R, you can then replicate that project in Python. Maybe you have a project in C++ or C# that you can port to Java or JavaScript.

When you finish, make an article about the Rosetta Stone that points to a GitHub repo. If you want to add one more technique, make a quick reference out of your Rosetta Stone.

Make a Quick Reference (Cheat Sheet)

This is a favorite of mine. I often assign these quick reference cheat sheet assignments to students in my statistics classes. I beg them to make the quick references a part of their professional portfolio online.

Making a quick reference accomplishes at least two important goals:

1. It adds a tangible artifact to your portfolio.
2. It gives value to others.

Here in Figure 7.2, I show a cheat sheet that provides a quick reference on how to interpret the coefficients of multiple different regression equation specifications. Similar to Figure 7.1 these cheat sheets (quick references) are abbreviated to make sure they show well in the pages of this book. For other examples see https://coaching.adamrossnelson.com/book_bonuses.

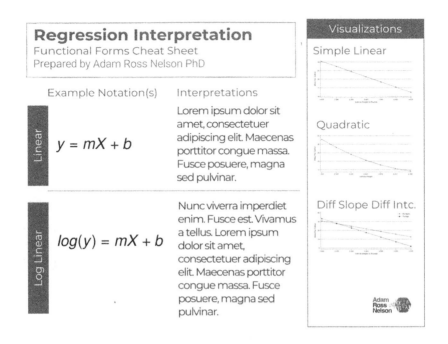

Figure 7.2

The best way to make a meaningful cheat sheet (or quick reference) is to make a list of topics, packages, techniques, tools, and other related items you know well. Then, start keeping notes on your most common tasks associated with those topics, packages, techniques, tools, and other related items.[13]

Another technique that can be helpful is to check your Google search history. Make a quick reference that provides information on what you repeatedly search for online. If you are searching for it, taking the time to make a quick reference will be beneficial for yourself. Likely, it will be beneficial to others, too.

---

[13] For useful quick reference or cheat sheet templates, go online to this book's bonuses at https://coaching.adamrossnelson.com/book_bonuses.

Write an Article about a Tool You Do Not Like

This is a variation on the more common advice of *write an article about a tool you like and use.*

Admittedly, this one is risky. Approach this option with care and caution. Be constructive with your feedback. Constructive feedback is input that offers useful ideas for improvements and updates. One of the better approaches will be to identify a tool, package, or feature that does not rise to meet its full potential. Explain what you see as the full potential and then describe steps that might help the tool better reach that full potential. An example of how I did this was to discuss the lack of output when performing a merge operation in Python (Nelson, 2020a).

Another example is when I discussed how moving columns around in Pandas is difficult (Nelson, 2020d). I identified the standard solutions and why they fell short of their full potential. Then I wrote about an alternate solution.

Convert Your Notes from Class into a Blog or an Article

As discussed in the chapters above, it is important for data scientists to continue the learning journey at every stage of career development. Blogging as you learn is both a great way to reinforce your learning and a way to be more efficient. During the learning process, it can be helpful to rewrite and reorganize your notes. If you convert your notes into blog posts, you accomplish two important objectives with a single task.

Firstly, you can share what you have learned with others. Secondly, you help to solidify the information in your own mind.

In addition, you will connect with other students and educators who are interested in the same topic.

Consider the following format or title options:

- Method A vs. Method B (How They Compare and When to Use Each)
- Pros + Cons of . . .
- How To . . .
- Lessons From . . .
- Getting Data From . . . : A Cookbook
- Getting Started with [Tool Name]: A Cookbook
- Having Fun with [Technique Name]: A Beginner's Guide
- X Things You Should Know About . . .
- Why [Tool Name] Is My Go-To For [Common Task]

Recruiter Ready GitHub

A collection of quality GitHub repositories can be a highly effective means of setting yourself above other job candidates. Early in the pandemic, in the midst of those toughest moments when everyone had to interact via Zoom, a colleague and I were discussing a recent review of one applicant pool that consisted of 200 applications. This review indicated that as few as 5% of applicants had taken the time to prepare a quality GitHub profile.

THE DISTRIBUTED PORTFOLIO STRATEGY

Let us define a quality GitHub profile. A quality profile has:

- At least three pinned repositories.
- A clear and well-organized ReadMe.md file for each pinned repository.

For more on what it means to have a clear and well-organized ReadMe.md file, see below.

Typically, recruiters may review your GitHub. They may even find you because of your GitHub. However, it will not be recruiters who will scrutinize your GitHub profile. Instead, it will be hiring managers and co-workers who will do the closer review of your profile.

You want an impressive GitHub profile for at least three reasons:

1. Recruiters will know a quality profile when they see one, even though recruiters will not likely scrutinize your GitHub profile. Quality profiles are not difficult to recognize.
2. Many hiring managers and co-workers will proactively search for your GitHub profile, even though some will not.
3. For those that do not proactively seek your GitHub profile, you want an opportunity to direct hiring managers and prospective co-workers toward your profile.

How Hiring Managers and Co-Workers Will View Your GitHub

Once on your GitHub, however they reach it, most prospective hiring managers and co-workers will visit your profile and do two things:

1. They will notice your contribution history (the green tiled visual).

   If you are currently employed, you should have a minimum of two to three commits per month. This is because someone working full time presumably commits to a private corporate git server—which is often not visible on your GitHub public profile. Thus, any publicly visible commits you may have will be on your own personal, hobby, or portfolio work.

   If you are fortunate enough that your work-related git commits are public, your git commits will be more plentiful. A plentiful git commit history is a strong plus for your profile.

   If you are unemployed, you should have a minimum of two to three git commits per week. Logically, someone who is unemployed but seeking work in data science should make frequent commits in the course of writing code for portfolio entries. Regardless of your current circumstances, an active and consistent git history shows that you are keeping your skills current and that you are active in the field.

2. They will browse your pinned repositories.

Many users will pick one of your pinned repositories to explore—hiring managers and co-workers may not have time for much more than that. For best results, you need a full ReadMe.md file. Many will not look past your ReadMe.md file. For this reason, devote as much time to your documentation as you do to your code. A collection of Jupyter notebooks is not sufficient.

There are roughly three factors that figure into a hiring manager's or prospective co-worker's decision on which repository to browse:

1. They will look at the titles. The first repository they will click will be the one with the most interesting title.
2. They will look at the languages. The next repository they will click will be the one that identifies a language used at that workplace.
3. Some may go directly to review the repository you specifically suggested they review.

A Clear + Well-Organized Readme.md

Overall, it is difficult to predict which of your pinned repositories will get the most views.

Each pinned repository should have a full ReadMe.md that is well organized. A clear and well-organized ReadMe.md includes headings, introductory paragraphs, bulleted lists, and enumerated instructions. To prepare your repositories, start with one that you believe showcases your skill and ability the best. Focus on grooming it to meet these specifications.

Get feedback from trusted friends. Another technique that can help you improve your profile is to request your online connections via LinkedIn, Facebook, and Twitter to review your profile and offer feedback. Take that feedback to make improvements. Once it is ready, pin it to your profile and then move on to another—but never stop seeking input. As further explained below ProWritingAid, Grammarly, other writing tools, or trusted friends who can proofread will help you avoid publishing spelling and grammatical errors.

Optimize Your Profile

In addition to the above factors and considerations, comb through your profile settings to optimize them for your job search. The following are best practices you should consider as you prepare and update your profile and its settings.

- Use your full name, and make sure it matches the name you use on LinkedIn and your resume.

- Displaying a public email address is optional. Displaying your email will make it easier for prospective employers to contact you. However, directing users to your LinkedIn will be sufficient and easier to manage.
- List an external URL in your profile. If you do not have your own website, give a direct link to your LinkedIn or Twitter.
- There is a place to list your Twitter username. Listing your Twitter here assumes you have one and that it reflects your professional interests. If your Twitter reflects hobbies not related to your current profession and professional aspirations, consider not listing your Twitter username.
- List your company if you are associated with one.
- List a location that matches your LinkedIn location. The rules for identifying your location are the same for GitHub as they are for LinkedIn (see the LinkedIn section in Chapter 6 for these rules).
- Configure your settings to display a PRO badge, if available to you. This badge was formerly available to paid users and those with a verified (.edu) email. GitHub continuously updates the range of features that are available.
- Configure your settings to display an Arctic Code Vault badge. And if you do not know what this Code Vault badge signifies, Google it and get up to speed on the topic! Or read about it here: archiveprogram. github.com. (A good read for sure).

- Check the box that says you are available for hire. Doing so will display jobs on your GitHub dashboard.
- Make sure you have a professional username. Your username will also be a part of your GitHub URL. If you think it may be wise to improve the professionalism of your username by changing it, first read about the possible ramifications of changing your username (GitHub Docs, 2022).

Optimize Your GitHub Bio

GitHub provides a space for you to write a brief biography. They call it a bio. Use this space. (The rules for this section on GitHub are similar to the rules for LinkedIn's about section as discussed in Chapter 6.)

- Make sure that your profile uses keywords associated with your desired professional role.
- Use this biographic space to highlight your accomplishments. Do not be shy.
- Do not write about aspirations in this section. Write about what you have done and what you do now.
- I recommend writing in first-person perspective.
- If you have public-facing work products stored on an external site (blog, personal website, corporate website, etc.), you can share links to them on the about section.

Optimize Your Repositories

Specific setting guidelines for each repository:

- Curate your repositories. This means keeping your repositories updated and refreshed on a semi-regular basis.
- Set draft, dated (stale), and undocumented repositories as private.
- Each pinned repository needs to be complete with a ReadMe.md file and a License.md file.
- Once you pin your repositories, you can decide in which order they will appear.
- Be sure your ReadMe.md files (and all of your markdown files and code documentation) are free of grammatical or typographic errors. Ask a friend to proofread or consider using ProWritingAid, Grammarly, or another writing tool.

Chapter Summary

Standing out during the application process is crucial when job hunting in today's market. Following Chapter 5 and 6, which outlined how to prepare traditional job documents for your transition, this chapter discussed how to approach building a professional portfolio across various social media platforms.

By using this distributed strategy, you will establish a strong persona as a professional data scientist, in addition to reminding folks about yourself through multiple avenues. Pursuing this distributed strategy will involve placing portfolio content within sites such as GitHub, Medium, Quora, and LinkedIn.

The type of portfolio entry will determine which site is the best to use. Oftentimes, you can craft multiple versions of an entry, each formatted for a different platform. Entries on one platform will support and reinforce entries on other platforms. Eventually, their cumulative worth grows to be greater than the simple sum of the individual components.

Creating content for your portfolio entries can seem overwhelming. However, you do not need to produce an entire portfolio all at once. You have time. And you should use your time to produce portfolio entries on a consistent basis. Consistency is more important than perfection.

A further relief from the somewhat intimidating notion of a distributed portfolio strategy is that if you have been interested in data science for some time, you may have already done at least some of the leg work. Do not overlook the work you have already put into becoming a data scientist. Looking back at your previous learning experiences means reviewing your work and using that work to devise portfolio entries.

If you continue to need sources of inspiration for portfolio entry ideas, this chapter listed several ideas and starting points for your use. Your portfolio will develop further the more you pursue what interests you.

CHAPTER 8

Communicating with Employers

This chapter will give specific guidance on the types of people you will encounter in the course of the job application, recruitment, and selection process. Knowing the types of people you will encounter will allow you to plan which questions to ask each type of person. There will be additional advice on the types of interviews you may encounter.

Asking questions shows that you have sufficient self-awareness to recognize what you do not yet know. The one who asks a question is a fool for a minute, while the one who never asks at all is a fool for life.

Analytical people (and mid- and late-career professionals) understand the importance of asking good questions for work-related purposes. This chapter is about applying the wisdom you have already acquired through the course of your career to the job interview process.

The first bit of advice I have regarding communicating with employers through the job interview process is to reframe the process in your mind. Think of the process less as an interview and more as a discussion. Consistent with this philosophy, notice the chapter title is "Communicating with Employers."

Let this chapter be your guide in understanding how to ask questions. Candidates who know how to ask questions well (and then apply the information gathered as useful insights) tend to do best when responding to employer questions during the interview process.

The main subsections of this chapter are: "Who Is Who in Data Science Recruitment," "Before the Interviews," and "During the Interviews." The following chapter discusses salary negotiation.

The "Who Is Who" section will help you understand the various characters you may encounter during the recruitment and selection process. Knowing who is who, and what role they play, will help you know who to ask when you have questions.

This chapter describes a range of interview types and roughly the kinds of knowledge, skills, and abilities employers will expect you to show in each interview type. The "During the Interviews" section outlines what you must share when meeting and interacting with prospective employers.

Who Is Who in Data Science Recruitment

Solving the "who is who" mystery is a serious challenge for mid- and late-career professionals seeking a transition from one field to another. Many mid- and late-career professionals have not recently changed jobs from one organization to another. Therefore, keep in mind that the recruiting and hiring processes have transformed in the last few decades. Discovering exactly what a recruiter does and how the recruiter interacts with the hiring manager provides a competitive advantage for candidates.

This section will provide practical advice on solving the "who is who" mystery. The first portion will walk readers through a list of common position titles, with descriptions of how the titles relate to others in the recruitment and selection process. Keep in mind that the nomenclature may vary from organization to organization. The second portion will offer specific advice on how to mine for "who is who" information at individual companies and organizations.

Internal Recruiter

From a candidate's perspective, internal recruiters are directly employed by prospective employers. The role of an internal recruiter is to partner with the hiring manager in finding, selecting, and acquiring the right candidate for open positions. Not only is the internal recruiter looking to hire the right candidate, but they are looking to hire someone quickly and affordably.

Sometimes, an internal recruiter needs to focus on removing organizational barriers that impede the process of hiring quickly and affordably. For example, if the hiring manager has no room in their calendar to meet with a prospective candidate, the internal recruiter may negotiate a solution that will allow that hiring manager to be more readily available for interviews. An internal recruiter usually has the authority, in consultation with others, to deprioritize open positions if or when a hiring manager is unable to fully participate in the selection process.

An internal recruiter knows the company and its culture well. They are well-informed on how the company's culture differs from one portion of the organization to the next. Not all organizations have a consistent culture from one operational area to another. An internal recruiter can be a valuable source of intelligence for candidates seeking to understand those nuances.

Many organizations compensate internal recruiters solely through base salary. Some organizations may also provide performance-based compensation as well. Internal recruiters may be, but are not always, eligible for annual bonuses. Usually, there are no bonuses for internal recruiters who hire candidates within a specific timeline or within a specific salary range.

External Recruiters

External recruiters are individuals, or a team of individuals, who serve as consultants for employers. The hiring organization is an external recruiter's client. Employers sometimes hire external recruiters to fill a single position or for a larger contract that may involve filling many positions.

Employers compensate external recruiters differently than internal recruiters. External recruiters often earn substantial commissions. Commission-based compensation for external recruiters is usually calculated as a percentage of the candidate's first year salary. This percentage can range widely from one organization to another or from one contract to another but 15%–25% is typical. This commission-based structure creates an incentive for external recruiters to identify and recruit candidates who will qualify for higher salaries. However, this commission-based structure also creates an incentive for employers to place strict limits on salary during the salary negotiation process. These counter-veiling incentives are important for candidates to keep in mind during the recruitment, selection, offer, and negotiation processes.

Because an external recruiter does not work within the hiring organization, they might have a limited view of the hiring organization's culture and hiring process. Therefore, it can be useful to know if you are interacting with an external recruiter so you can ask that recruiter how long they have worked with the employer. If you learn an external recruiter has not worked with the employer for very long, you will need to enhance your efforts to learn about the organization's culture from sources beyond the external recruiter.

Hiring Managers

The hiring manager will supervise the employee once hired. This often means that the hiring manager will have a role in on-boarding and employee orientation. Relationships with hiring managers may have lasting and long-term implications for a candidate's career advancement and development.

During the recruitment and selection process, hiring managers partner with a recruiter, either internal or external, to find the right fit for the manager's team. The hiring manager defines the role in a manner that the recruiter can articulate as a job description. The recruiter will then use this job description when identifying candidates in resume banks and other candidate databases.

A hiring manager desires to support their team and produce results for the organization while being cognizant of their team's budget. Failed searches are costly. Therefore, the hiring manager is sensibly motivated to offer competitive salaries, but not overly competitive. The hiring manager's primary motivation is to acquire an individual with the set of skills needed among their existing team—or an individual with the ability to acquire these necessary skills swiftly.

The hiring manager is going to have answers to questions regarding a day in the life of working in your new role. As the hiring manager has a role in defining the job's expectations and responsibilities, they will also have credible answers to questions related to expectations and responsibilities.

During the interview process, the hiring manager may have a role in preparing others who will interview you. In a well-designed hiring process, and in the best-case scenario, a hiring manager will receive and review feedback from others who interview you through the recruitment and selection process.

Search Committee

This is a term whose meaning varies from organization to organization. Instead of *search committee*, some employers might choose the term *search panel*, *selection panel*, or another term with similar connotations.

Academic settings and organizations have a reputation for utilizing search committees. Many organizations utilize search committees for executive roles within an organization as well.

From the employer's perspective, a search committee provides several advantages. First, when implemented correctly, a search committee can help to ensure that all candidates are given equal consideration. This fairness is especially important for roles that are highly competitive or contested. Second, a search committee can help to ensure there is a breadth of input—that a diverse selection of the organization's stakeholders have a say in who is ultimately selected for the role. Achieving this breadth of input also requires a well-designed and implemented process. This breadth of input is important because it helps to ensure the organization's values and objectives are taken into account when making the final decision. Finally, a search committee can help to provide a sense of objectivity in the assessment of candidates. This objectivity matters because it leads to hiring decisions that are based on merit, rather than on personal connections or bias.

From the candidate's perspective, after the recruiter or the hiring manager, a search committee may be the bulk of who they will meet in an interview process. As such, a search committee can provide an opportunity for candidates to meet members from across the organization—people who might not otherwise have been involved in the interview process, such as cross-functional peers and external partners.

Ideally, all members of a search committee will meet every candidate. However, sometimes one or more members of a search committee will miss an interview. In these cases, it is not uncommon for employers to video or audio record search committee interviews for absent members to review at a later time.

After completing interviews, search committee members often individually submit reviews to the hiring manager. Based on the input from the search committee, and other factors including the manager's own experiences with candidates during the search and selection process, it will then be the hiring manager's role to select which candidate to hire.

Hiring Panel

Think of a hiring panel as a variation on a search committee. Where the role of a search committee is limited to providing input to a hiring manager on a collection of candidates, the role of a hiring panel can be more specific. Instead of providing general feedback on each candidate, a hiring panel may recommend or decide which specific candidate to hire.

Hiring panel members may vote, aiming for a consensus so that they can collectively recommend a specific candidate to the hiring manager. A search committee may recommend a specific candidate for hire or a group of finalists from which the hiring manager will make a final selection.

It is useful for a candidate to understand whether an employer is using a search committee, a hiring panel, or some variation. When candidates know they will interact with a search committee or hiring panel, it is wise to ask for clarification on what role the panel or committee performs in the recruitment and selection process. Possessing specific knowledge regarding the role a panel or committee performs will assist candidates as they respond to questions in the recruitment and selection process.

Recruiting Coordinator

A recruiting coordinator is another individual you may meet along your way through the interview process. Recruiting coordinators may have very basic information about the role for which you are interviewing. Their primary role in the interview process is to handle logistics. Often secretarial, executive assistants, or other support staff will serve in the role of a recruiting coordinator. As a candidate, you can think of the recruiting coordinator as a point of contact to help with scheduling, parking, Zoom meeting credentials, contact information for others involved in the search, interview related travel expenses, and general communications.

A recruiting coordinator will work with your recruiter and hiring manager to schedule and organize your interview. If your interview is in person, the recruiting coordinator may be the person who will meet you at the door, validate your parking, give you a tour of the facility or office, offer you a beverage, show you the restroom, help you locate gender neutral restrooms, and otherwise help you navigate the day. For example, when in doubt the recruiting coordinator could also help direct you to the correct conference room or office for each portion of your interview experience. If your interview is virtual, the recruiting coordinator will ensure you have the correct virtual meeting link and assist in troubleshooting if necessary. A recruiting coordinator can also be helpful in providing other contact information for those with whom you may wish to communicate before, during, and after the recruitment and selection process.

Compensation Team

The compensation team is another group that may be involved in a candidate's offer. Usually, the compensation team operates behind the scenes. In this case, operating behind the scenes means that candidates will not directly interact with the compensation team members. Candidates will often not interact with compensation team members directly. Instead, compensation team members work with the recruiter and hiring manager to determine what amount to offer a candidate, which is based on the candidate's experience as well as how the company compensates similar employees. The compensation team may subscribe to databases that provide compensation benchmark intelligence, which can be influential in the salary negotiation processes.

When an organization employs a compensation team, it is not cause for concern if a recruiter or hiring manager requires multiple days to respond or counter a candidate's request for a higher salary than what the initial offer listed. Avoid worrying if it takes the recruiter a few days to get back to you with an answer; they are likely working with the compensation team to determine what additional compensation they may (or may not) add to your offer. Compensation practices vary widely from organization to organization. Sometimes, your hiring manager may influence your final offer. However, in other instances, the hiring manager's input may be much more subordinate to the compensation team's input.

Obtaining an Organizational Chart

Obtaining an organizational chart from one or more of your prospective employers is a swift technique that can help you further solve the "who is who" problem. When you find the right organizational chart, you will specifically solve the "who is who" problem at your specific organization of interest.

Many organizations make some version of their organizational chart available online. When a company provides a list of employees (but not in the form of an organizational chart), it can be a useful exercise to draw out an organizational chart based on the information you have. Drawing out that organizational chart will help familiarize yourself with the company.

If you are unsure where to start in building an organizational chart, and the organization of interest makes no organizational chart available (on a public website), you can ask for one. Requesting an organizational chart from the recruiter or HR professional is a sensible step. I find it is better to ask this kind of question early on in the process of speaking with recruiters. I try to ask when I am on the phone. I say, "By the way, do you have an organizational chart handy? I would be so happy to review the organizational chart if you have that available?"

Another option is to find an organizational chart for an organization that is similar to the one in which you are interested. Similar organizations tend to structure themselves similarly. Another smart reason to review organizational charts from similar organizations is that doing so can build your awareness of your target company's area of practice, niche, subspeciality, etc. Demonstrating your knowledge on similar (or competing) organizations to your prospective employer will help you in the discussion process during recruitment and selection.

Another resource to consider is The Org (https://theorg. com). This website collects and provides organizational charts for thousands of organizations across the world. At the time of a recent check, The Org listed nearly 30,000 organizations with under 50 employees. Thus, if this site cannot find the organizational chart for your specific organization of interest, it will locate organizational charts from other similar organizations.

Of course, it would be easier if every job listing contained that company's organizational chart. Or, if every employer maintained and provided their organizational chart for prospective employees' reference. This *organizational chart distribution as standard*, however, is not the case for most employers. Even if an employer provides you with an organizational chart, consider seeking and reviewing other organizational charts on your own. The differences between what a recruiter supplies and what you find on your own can be informative for you.

The last bit of advice on solving the "who is who" problem at your organization of interest is to keep looking for more structural information even after you have found an organizational chart. You may find multiple organizational charts. Each chart might be slightly different and provide subtle, or not so subtle, insights for you. For example, comparing older organizational charts with newer organizational charts can help you understand how the organization has evolved.

Looking over long-term organizational evolution through their organizational charts helps you understand how employees advance (or do not advance) in the organization. Another savvy reason to research companies by reviewing their past and present organizational charts is that you will learn about the history of the organization beyond what they publish online or in written reports. When you learn, and then show, this fine-grain knowledge of an employer, you show that you have strong research skills. By using this technique, candidates may even know more about the organization's history than those who are asking questions in the interviews.

Once you have the organizational chart, there will be components or aspects of the organization that might not fully make sense to you. Make notes of the questions that come to your mind so you can ask those questions at the right time and place later in the recruitment and selection process. An impressive way to show your homework is to demonstrate information that the prospective employer may not be aware of—or may not have recently contemplated.

The best organizational charts will include the title and the name of the person currently in the role you seek (or in a similar role). Having the name and title of current or former employees in the role you seek can help you understand where others came from prior to having that role, and where they have gone after having that role.

This career ladder information is useful as you plan for salary negotiations. Knowing this kind of information can prompt you to ask more well-informed versions of the question: "What advancement opportunities are there for candidates in this role?"

Many job postings in data science will not reveal the name of the hiring manager, which will probably be surprising for mid- and late-career professionals transitioning into tech or data science (or for those who have not participated in a job search recently). A good organizational chart can help you uncover information about the job description's unmentioned hiring manager. If it does not identify the specific hiring manager, it might identify a range of possibilities. This intelligence can help you further research the employment history and backgrounds of other employees working for that organization and in your targeted portion of that organization. Such information will be invaluable at all stages of the recruitment and selection process. For example, if the position asks for a cover letter, this information will help you connect with your readers in personalized ways.

Organizational charts can sometimes provide cautionary information. Seeking, observing, and asking questions about cautionary information, such as excessive vacancies or excessive turnover, is another important communication objective during the recruitment and selection process. Empty spots can also signal opportunities for advancement.

Before the Interviews

Before the interview is when you spend your time and energy planning what you want to know about the employer's recruitment processes, their expectations for you should they decide to hire you, and what they offer as an employer. You need to ask questions throughout the course of your interview process, and a great way to make sure you ask the right kinds of questions in the right ways is to plan ahead for each interview type.

Predicting exactly the types of interviews you will encounter in any given job search is not quite possible. However, you can make an educated guess based on the experience of others. Likewise, precisely predicting the types of knowledge, skills, and abilities an employer may ask you to show in any given interview is also difficult.

The surest way to know what kind of interviews you will encounter and the types of knowledge, skills, and abilities an employer may want you to show is to ask. There are risks associated with asking questions: You could seem foolish, unaware, unready, or clueless. However, when done well, asking questions will make you seem the opposite. Asking the right kinds of questions, at the right times, in the right ways, and with sufficient background knowledge will reveal you as informed, well-prepared, and perceptive.

As listed below, there are at least 12 types of interviews you might expect while applying for a job in data science.

Use the outline of interview types presented here as a general guide in preparing for each interview type. However, a sure way to know what type of skills, abilities, and knowledge you should work to show in each type of interview is to ask the prospective employer. Recall how the interview process is a discussion. For any employer worth working for, it is never off-limits to ask questions. Often, employers will even say, "Do you have any questions for us before we get started today?" Or the recruiter might say, "Let me know if you have any questions before you arrive for your interview."

A candidate might avoid asking questions for fear of appearing unaware, inexperienced, or unsavvy. Avoiding questions (for those reasons) is a mistake.

In the context of a conversation, a smart question for a candidate to ask might sound like:

> **Candidate:** *For the technical interview we have coming up, will there be a focus on probability or statistics (theory)? Or perhaps a close look at specific tools and technologies (practical)? Perhaps you know if it will be a mix of both?*

Recruiter: *I can check with the team on that for you. Help me understand your specific questions a bit better.*

Another scenario could be:

Candidate: *Will you assign an assessment via an online screening platform?*

Recruiter: *Yes, we use a variety of platforms for this, including Code Submit, Code Signal, iMochi, Coding Game, and Coder Byte. I would be glad to get you more specifics on that, so watch your email.*

If a candidate is seeking more information about a product sense interview, the following question would be appropriate:

Candidate: *Every team and company will approach product sense in a different way. In advance of that interview, can you help me get a better understanding of your team's philosophy?*

Another example of a scenario you might face is one in which the employer asks you to complete a product sense interview but does not call it a product sense interview. The employer might call it a *planning workshop*. If your interview is called a planning workshop, and there is no clear indication as to what that means, you might ask more questions. For example:

Candidate: *I do not believe I am familiar with the 'planning workshop' interview format. Can you help me understand what the planning workshop will involve?*

Or the employer might not call their interviews anything specific at all. The employer might just show you a list of interviews with names of the people you will meet without any real indication of the topics for each meeting or the type of format. In this case, a good question might be:

Candidate: *Did you plan a product sense interview? I do not see one listed here. Will any of these focus on product sense?*

Asking the question will open the opportunity for you to discuss the process and gather useful information on how to prepare for your interviews. Asking the question also signals that you are paying close attention to the interview process and that you are thinking strategically about how you can help them best evaluate you as a candidate. Many employers will regard this brand of strategic thinking as a professional asset.

Types of Interviews in Data Science

Below is a list of interview styles or formats candidates may encounter in the data science job search. Use this list to familiarize yourself with the range of interview styles. When you speak with recruiters and recruiting coordinators, you can ask them to explain what kinds of interviews you should expect.

Technical

Technical interviews, for data science positions, will often involve one or more of the following specific topics:

> ➤ Writing code (Python, R, SQL, or similar).
> ➤ Algorithmic thought (such as solving the well-known "fizz buzz" coding challenge or devising an algorithm that efficiently produces the sum of all odd numbers ranging from 1 to 100).
> ➤ Debugging existing code.
> ➤ Refactoring existing code.
> ➤ Interpreting statistical output (explaining the results of a regression).
> ➤ Data visualization (planning, presenting, or improving a visual analysis, such as converting a pie chart to a proportionally stacked bar chart or adding data labels to an existing data visual example).
> ➤ Data prep (preparing data for a specific analytical technique, such as generating an array of one-hot encoded categorical variables).

I enjoy technical interviews. Sure, for newer data scientists, they might feel like an opportunity to reveal yourself as a newbie. They might even feel like an opportunity for employers to identify candidates who have overstated their skills. And if I am being honest, technical interviews perform both of those intimidating functions. The risk, of course, is that they can produce a false positive. A technical interview may show a candidate as someone who overstated their skills, while the truth is that the candidate merely had a bad moment and normally would have produced a smart, workable, or even flawless solution.

However, among employers who implement technical interviews well, they are actually aimed at understanding how the candidate solves problems within the specific sets of platforms, tools, and techniques often used by other employees at the organization.

Many of the guidelines that apply to other forms of interviews also apply during a technical interview. Unless the interviewer has specifically said, "For this portion of the interview, we want you to work independently without assistance from others" (which they could say), treat the technical interview as a discussion.

Preparing for a technical interview involves practicing your coding, data management, and problem-solving skills. Five well-known online platforms that help candidates prepare for technical interviews are: DataLemur (https://datalemur.com), Select Star SQL (https://selectstarsql.com), the SQL Murder Mystery video game (https://mystery.knightlab.com), LeetCode (https://leetcode.com), and Daily Coding Problem (https://www.dailycodingproblem.com). There are also smart phone apps such as Mimo (https://getmimo.com).

On DataLemur, one of the newest resources on this list, you will find practice SQL interview questions as asked by a variety of highly sought-after and appealing tech employers. According to its website, Select Star SQL provides "An interactive book which aims to be the best place on the internet for learning SQL. It is free of charge, free of ads, and doesn't require registration or downloads." Finally, the Murder Mystery site explains that you are working in a hypothetical scenario where "a crime has taken place and the detective needs your help. The detective gave you the crime scene report, but you somehow lost it . . . You vaguely remember that the crime was a murder that occurred sometime on Jan 15, 2018, and that it took place in SQL City." On this platform, your first task is to find the crime scene report from the fictional police station data. From there the mission continues, should you choose to accept it.

Whiteboard

A whiteboard interview is a special kind of technical interview that includes the use of a whiteboard (or pen and paper, a chalkboard, or other place to write out thoughts and ideas). If an interviewer asks you to write code on a whiteboard, you are probably in some kind of whiteboard interview.

Whiteboard interviews are becoming more and more popular as tech companies try to assess a candidate's problem-solving skills. Because the whiteboard interview is a special kind of technical interview (possibly indistinguishable from a technical interview, depending on the employer's specific instructions or setup), you can aim to make the experience as conversational as the interviewers will allow.

The goal of a whiteboard interview is for the interviewer to see your thought processes. The whiteboard will make visible what you think of first, second, and third. The interview will reveal how you sequence and prioritize your problem-solving processes.

An effective way to prepare for a whiteboard interview is to practice with an actual whiteboard. If you can, ask the recruiter or recruiting coordinator how big your whiteboard will be, if it will be an actual whiteboard, and how many others will be there. Find a way to match those conditions, and then practice under those conditions. In practice, and then later in the interview itself, be sure to speak out loud about each step, figure, equation, code block, or other item you draw on the whiteboard. Speaking out loud can help interviewers better understand your thought process, as they cannot read your mind.

Product Sense

During a product sense interview, the employer will usually look for your ability to perform well within one or more areas of thought. You should be able to identify which features may be missing as well as opportunities for new product features. An insightful thought to offer within a product sense interview would be an idea for a feature that has not yet been announced but that would benefit product users. You will know you have done well on offering that form of insight when the employer responds during the interview with a comment that sounds like "There is an idea we have not yet considered. Tell us more, please?" Or perhaps even better, "We agree with you, and we have work related to building that feature in our plans, but we have not yet begun that work." A product sense interview is an opportunity for the product owner to evaluate how well you can help them in planning future developments for their products.

When preparing for this type of interview, keep in mind that the product owner is your intended audience. If the customer success team has produced trainings, webinars, blog posts, or video tutorials, you should review those materials and take copious amounts of notes. The customer success and customer onboarding materials will be one of the fastest ways for you to learn about the product (other than actually using it). In a manner of speaking, many product sense interview questions have the answers already published online in the customer success, onboarding, or other general resources related to the product. If the product you will work on does not have customer success training materials, you can benefit from reviewing the customer success training materials from the product's competitors.

Another important element of product sense is demonstrating a firm understanding of the product's typical user. For particularly niche products, the avatar of the product's ideal user could be quite specific. You should understand what the typical user's main problems are and how the product aims to solve one or more of those problems. The more you know about the product's typical user, the more equipped you will be at demonstrating a strong sense of the product.

Behavioral

Recruiting involves psychology. This means that behavioral interviews are among the most common interviews. In a behavioral interview, you talk about how you have behaved in the past. The interview might feel like a conversation, but it is important to give specific details when talking about your own past behavior. Employers are looking for evidence that will show your style related to communication, decisiveness, leadership, teamwork, and resilience.

They will ask you about a process that led to a specific outcome. For example, "Tell us about a time when something at work was not going as expected or desired, perhaps a time when you were up against a hard deadline, and you thought you might not deliver on time?" Or "Was there ever a time when you had to learn a new tool or technology quickly that you can tell us about?" As a candidate, you must be prepared to speak in detail about the actions you took and what you learned along the way. You should also be sure to give details related to the outcomes your team or organization experienced as a result of your actions.

The situation, task, action, result mnemonic acronym (STAR) tends to work well in a behavioral interview:

(**S**) Begin by speaking about the **situation** that you faced.
(**T**) Then speak about the **task** that was at hand.
(**A**) Describe the **action** you took.

(**R**) Lastly, outline the **result** that happened due to your action.[14]

Be honest; tell true stories. A good way to prepare for this kind of interview is to write out how you would respond to specific questions and then rehearse what you wrote. Another excellent technique is to practice with a trusted colleague, interview coach, or career coach.

Conversational

In a conversational interview, the interviewer will ask you questions about your experience and what you know about the job. They want to assess how you respond, how relaxed you are, your personality, and whether you would be a good fit for the company. This is normally done in a one-on-one setting, but it can also be done informally with a group of people.

When you go for a conversational interview, it is important to remember that it is a conversation. You should still plan what you want to say in advance, but do not worry if you do not get to say everything you planned on saying because there will be other chances later.

Direct

When there are many candidates, it is easier for the employer to compare those candidates by including a direct interview.

---

[14] For more information related to this S.T.A.R. acronym see this book's online bonus resources at https://coaching.adamrossnelson.com/book_bonuses.

In this kind of interview, they will ask all of the candidates the same questions. This can be hard on a candidate, but there will be other opportunities to show creativity and free thought.

Throughout this kind of interview, it is useful to recall the questions being asked. Soon after this interview, write out what you remember of the questions and how you responded. Use those notes as you participate in later interviews. These notes will be helpful to you as you think of what questions you will want to ask later in the interview process.

They direct this interview toward comparing many candidates to reduce the number of candidates under consideration. Therefore, if you do not advance in the selection process following a direct interview, just know that you may have been the victim of a numbers game. Stay acquainted with the folks you met in the course of a direct interview. Through these connections, you may learn about future opportunities. Remaining in contact with these new acquaintances can also build your familiarity which may favor you in subsequent interviews for other job listings.

Case Study

In this kind of interview, the employer will offer you an overview of a *case*. A case is a moderately complicated business scenario related to an entire organizational unit, or sometimes an entire organization. The timeframe of the business problem will likely be long ranged.

A useful technique is to repeat back what you believe the case involves. Doing so allows you to demonstrate an important skill that employers look for in an interview—your ability to listen. It is likewise important to ask specific questions for elaboration and clarification.

For example, a common case interview scenario is for candidates to devise an evaluation plan. The case will ask candidates to specify how to collect data and then analyze that data so the organization can determine how successful a program, product feature, or initiative has been. In such case interviews, a good question is "Have you decided how to define success? Or, are you looking for me to do that step?" Make sure your response will measure what the interviewers consider important to measure.

When the case interview is live and on the spot, another technique that demonstrates a good skill is to ask "Do you mind if I have a moment to make some notes and think about how I'd like to approach this?" If the case interview occurs in a take-home format, then you will have the opportunity to think and make your notes, anyway. However, asking to take a moment to organize your thoughts (when it makes sense to do so) will demonstrate the intention you bring to your deliberation process.

Ultimately, interviewers will look for a structured approach to addressing the questions presented, plus a well-communicated summary of that approach. The goal for candidates is to identify a path forward even though the employer's given scenario does not clearly point to a specific path. When proposing a path forward, a candidate reveals their ability to think through a problem and definitively arrive at a path forward that will likely produce meaningful results, even when there is no clear standard approach or solution.

Practical

The practical interview is a type of interview that is used to assess a candidate's pragmatic problem-solving skills. The employer will present a specific business problem that their business is facing, or may face in the future. The practical interview addresses nuances that conversational, or even behavioral, interviews might miss. This type of interview is common for technical roles, such as data science. Unlike the broad in scope, organization-wide, or long-term planning problems presented in a case study interview, the practical interview business problem will be much more moderate in scope.

The candidate's job is to diagnose the problem and identify potential solutions. There will be many adequate solutions. Few, if any, of the solutions will be obscure. What employers are looking for is your ability to articulate the problem, identify solutions, and then rank those solutions.

In subsequent interviews following a practical interview, a favorite technique of mine is to ask for the interviewers to reflect on the problem they had presented during that practical interview. I like to ask how subsequent interviewers might have diagnosed the problem, what solutions they saw, and which solution they might have selected.

Stress

It is no secret that job interviews can be stressful, anyway. Moreover, you might have heard of job interviews where the employer seemingly intentionally places the candidates in a stressful situation. Some recruiters believe this type of stress-testing can be a good way to see how candidates will react under pressure.

An example that I know of (but am not a fan of because I see it as manipulative) is for an employer to arrange for an interview in a room that is intentionally short on enough chairs for all anticipated attendees. This shortage of chairs induces stress for the candidates because it is an unanticipated situation, and the candidates will be a part of the solution (for example, by retrieving a chair from a nearby room).

Other tactics that might induce stress are to ask highly unanticipated questions, aggressive questions, or brain teasers.

Unanticipated question: *What was the first book you ever read?*

Aggressive question: *We also have a job opening for* [insert other random job position]. *Do you not think you should have applied for that job instead?*

Another aggressive stressor could be to offer negative feedback on one or more of your responses or on your behavior during the interview.

Brain teaser (or outright unanswerable) question: *What am I thinking right now? What would you be thinking if you were me, right now, in this situation?*

By putting candidates in a difficult situation, employers can get a better sense of their problem-solving skills and ability to think on their feet. Of course, it is important to strike a balance. As a candidate, if you feel an employer has placed you in a stress interview, consider asking for a lifeline. If you feel stressed, ask for a break. If something is not clear, ask for clarification. If you need or want help, ask for help. Remember that part of managing stress is knowing how to recognize stress and then finding support to manage that stress.

Meals

An interview that is conducted during a meal differs from any other interview. There are a few things you need to think about before this type of interview. If you can find the restaurant menu ahead of time, scope out an order choice that will be easy to eat. If you have food or meal restrictions, and if the recruiter has not asked you about those restrictions ahead of time, consider reaching out to the restaurant directly before your interview. Knowing what the restaurant can do to accommodate you ahead of time will reduce your stress, allowing you to focus on this opportunity to ask and answer questions in a less structured environment.

Whether consciously or not, the interviewer will observe how you interact with the host and the way you address the serving staff and other people in the restaurant. It is important to be polite to everyone in this situation.

When you are at a meal interview, connect the conversation with other interviews. This might sound something like: "I thought the case study you presented in the case interview cleverly included a nuance related to the costs of customer acquisition. The topic of customer acquisition costs came to my mind as an important aspect of that case. Can you tell me more about how you developed that case?" Or "I was having a good time, believe it or not, in the technical interview. I was not ready to have it be over. Is the problem you presented in that technical interview rooted in a specific experience you recently faced as an organization?"

Panel

In this interview format, the employer will ask a candidate to appear before a group or committee. Members of the group or committee will typically introduce themselves and their role in the organization. Following introductions, each member of the panel will ask questions, which they usually scripted ahead of time. These questions will be similar to the kinds of questions in the direct interview format.

From the perspective of the employer, the cynical goal of a panel interview is to minimize the risk of a *bad hire*. A bad hire could either mean selecting a candidate who does not meet expectations or selecting a candidate for impermissible reasons.

In a panel interview, you may face questions that resemble questions otherwise associated with product sense, whiteboard, behavioral, conversational, direct, case study, practical, stress, or any combination of these interview types.

Group

In contrast to the panel format of multiple interviewers and one candidate, a group interview involves multiple candidates. For employers, the goal of a group interview is to see how candidates interact with others.

The group interview is equally an opportunity for employers to see how candidates advocate for themselves while also making space to let others shine. Employers want to see candidates who can share the spotlight in a group interview. A classic question candidates might face in a group interview is: "Why are you interested in working here?" Given the fact that some candidates will speak before others, this question grows more difficult to answer over time—candidates will want to avoid sounding repetitive.

Employers can assess how candidates speak with others on unfamiliar topics by asking a question such as "We would like everyone here today to have a few moments to share about a topic that is complicated, but they know well. It will be an opportunity to share your passion. But also remember that time is limited as we go around the room. Would anyone care to go first?"

During the Interviews

There are at least two well-known acronyms / mnemonic devices designed to help candidates through a job interview. The first is the STAR method. The so-called STAR method (also discussed above) teaches you to respond to questions, especially behavioral interview questions, with a specific **situation** you have faced. Then discuss the **task** and **action** that you implemented as a result of that situation. Finally, conclude with an overview of the **results** you, your team, and your organization experienced because of the task and action.

Another popular mnemonic (frequently attributed to Google) is the XYZ template. This XYZ template teaches you to frame responses to most questions by showing how you accomplished [X] as measured by [Y] and by doing [Z].

For more references on this topic, including a workbook that you can use to prepare responses consistent with the STAR framework, visit: https://coaching.adamrossnelson.com/book_bonuses.

Acronyms and mnemonics aside, here are a list of eight things I teach candidates to show through the course of their interviews.

That You Listen Well

This list starts with listening and communication. In job interviews, recruiters are looking for candidates who can listen well and understand what others are saying. The ability to communicate effectively can make the difference between getting a job offer and being passed over for another candidate.

Listening is where good communication starts. Candidates who cannot listen well or do not understand what others are saying will likely have trouble communicating. Likewise, those who do not listen effectively will find it difficult to advance in their career. The good news about this skill, and all the skills on this list, is that you can learn it and improve upon it. If you want to be successful in today's job market, make sure you brush up on your listening skills so you can show this as a skill of yours in your job interviews.

That You Can Contribute to Sales

After learning a whole new field, data science, you might feel intimidated by the prospect of also learning to communicate your ability, and willingness, to contribute to a company's sales processes. As you prepare for interviews, make sure you take notes related to how the employer makes money. Show that you know how the company makes money and that you are enthused to contribute directly to the bottom line by supporting the employer's sales processes.

When interviewing with organizations that are not driven by profit make sure you understand the organization's revenue sources. The most successful data scientists, in one way or another, will often have a role in contributing positively to the organization's bottom line. Data science should be a profit or revenue center instead of a cost center. Showing your willingness and ability to serve as a source of revenue will help you in the interview process.

Your interviewers do not expect you to show that you are a sales genius. Instead, you merely need to show that you are cognizant of the importance of sales and the employer's bottom line, and that you are eager to support that bottom line through data science.

Some employers may ask specifically about sales. If you encounter a question that is about sales, do not punt on your response. Be sure to practice at least one full-throated response on how you can contribute to an employer's bottom and that you understand how even data scientists can and should contribute directly to that bottom line.

That You Are a Problem Solver

Problem-solving is one of the most important skills that you can possess in both your personal and professional life. As a result, problem-solving is something that is highly valued by employers and recruiters.

This item connects with the first item, listening, because if you know how to listen to someone's problem, you will have an advantage as you look over solutions to that problem.

To show your acumen in solving problems, speak about your resourcefulness, flexibility, and creativity. Show that you are solution-oriented. To get the job, which is the purpose of job interviews, candidates must show that they can effectively solve problems. An example of how you show yourself as solution oriented is when you or your team experience a delay or impasse. Of course, in such cases of delay or impasse, it is important to notify other stakeholders including managers. However, when you pair the notification with a list of next steps you intend to pursue, you show that you have anticipated what solutions may work to move the team past the delay or impasse. The focus on potential solutions reveals you as a solution oriented professional.

Problem-solving is an essential skill for anyone who wants to advance in their career in any field. Those who can find creative solutions to tough challenges are usually the ones who receive promotions and more responsibilities. In anticipation of that career advancement, it is important to present a strong first impression, including a sense that you are an effective problem solver.

That You Understand Specific, Job-Related, Technical Skills

This one often intimidates candidates. Do not misread this requirement as saying you must show a *complete* understanding of *all* technical skills, methods, or techniques available throughout the entire field of data science. Most employers intrinsically understand they need to provide some level of training for nearly all hires. You merely need to have a firm understanding of some specific, job-related, technical skills.

For example, you might *currently* be a specialist in logistic regression and linear regression modeling. You might *right now* be well versed in k-nearest neighbors and random forest classification techniques. However, you might also be *still learning* how to process audio data.

Make sure you know what you know. Make sure you understand what you are still learning. Communicate your levels of professional development with the right mix of confidence and humility.

That You Are Good at Math

Besides having a firm understanding of specific, job-related, technical skills, you need to show that you are good at math and quantitative reasoning more generally.

Throughout the world of data science career coaching, a pet peeve of mine is when anyone overstates the simplicity of becoming or working as a data scientist. I am always careful to never overstate the simplicity of any major accomplishment— or the acquisition of any important skill. Be cautious of anyone who offers advice that suggests you do not need to be good at math to excel in this field.

Mathematic skills will come more naturally for some than for others. No, you do not need to be an Albert Einstein level of genius at math. But, you do need a measure of practiced, current, and fresh skills with numbers.

An important caveat here is that there is a difference between experiencing a learning disability such as dyslexia or dyscalculia and being bad at math. I suffer from dyslexia and dyscalculia. As a result of these disabilities, many told me, and I falsely believed them, that I was bad at math. It was only later in my life that I learned how I am good at math. As these disabilities persist in who I am, I have to work (and work hard) to maintain my measure of practiced, current, and fresh skills with numbers. I am not one for whom this comes easily.

That You Are a Rock Star Communicator

In today's job market, communication skills are more important than ever. Recruiters are looking for candidates who can express themselves clearly and confidently in job interviews. Furthermore, employers want employees who can effectively communicate with customers, clients, and colleagues. This item is about making sure you can help others understand your thoughts and ideas.

In a data science role, which necessarily involves generating ideas and solving complex problems, the ability to convey complex thoughts and ideas in a manner that is accessible for others will set you ahead of other candidates.

That You Are a Star Communication Facilitator

Being a rock star communicator is not sufficient. You must also be a star in the communication facilitation role. The *star* analogy works well for this item on the *must show* list for job candidates during the interview because being a star means that others will look to you as a role model and source of inspiration.

Notice how communication shows up on this list in multiple ways. For example, the previous item was about being able to communicate your own ideas—about helping others understand your own thoughts and ideas. As a communication facilitator, you must show that you are good at helping others understand each other and that you are good at helping others express themselves. Being a strong communication facilitator is about guiding others in forming and building stronger mutual and common understandings.

That You Are Business Savvy and Solution-Oriented

For the last item on this list, remember that in today's job market, it is not enough to be qualified for a position. With many candidates vying for the same jobs, employers are looking for candidates who have that extra something which sets them apart from the rest. I may summarize this extra quality that makes a candidate stand out as business savvy.

Being solution-oriented is an important part of business savvy. These two traits pair together. One can demonstrate the other. Show that you possess business savvy and acumen by being solution-oriented. Being solution-oriented means that when a problem arises, you have the capacity to come up with creative and effective solutions. It also means you have the capacity to select the most appropriate solution, inform others around you of the problem, the available solutions, and the path you intend to take moving forward. Employers value people who can think quickly and critically solve challenges.

So instead of going to the team saying, "the cost for the tool that supports our recommendation engine is about to double and we will need a solution." You would say "he team, I have been tracking the costs of the tools that support our recommendation engine. The cost is about to go up. The way I see it there are three solutions. The solution I propose is [insert solution]. Also, here I have prepared some information that will help us lay the groundwork if we do decide as a team to move forward as I've recommended here."

Business savvy and acumen demonstrates to a potential employer that you have the skills, abilities, and desire to see yourself succeed, but also that you want the organization to succeed. While there are many qualities that can make a job candidate stand out, being business savvy, business-minded, and solution-oriented are especially important.

What Questions Do You Have for Us?

Most interviews will include some time for candidates to ask a handful of questions. They will ask, "What questions do you have for us?"

Responding to this question can be difficult. By following this book's advice, you have already asked a range of questions before you reach the concluding interview question of "What questions do you have for us?" Even if you feel you could have asked more questions along the way, it is not too late to redeem yourself by now showing that you can anticipate and ask quality, insightful questions.

And even in cases where you have already asked questions (hopefully) along the way, it continues to be important to do so (when prompted). This will show that you are fully engaged in the process and the conversation through to the conclusion of the interview experience.

Remember, the first piece of advice is to avoid waiting for the invitation to ask questions. If all has gone well, by the time employers invite you to ask questions, you have already asked several questions through the course of the interview and other communications with the employer. Below are two sources of inspiration for you as you think about what questions to ask. An added benefit of these sources of inspiration is that they can be easy to remember when you are at the end of the interview, low on energy, and possibly also feeling the (positive, negative, and overall disorienting) effects of the interview experience.

You Can Reuse the Employer's Questions

One technique to use when prompted to ask questions is to reuse questions from earlier in the interview. You can reuse questions that were asked of you. You can also reuse questions that you asked of them.

Here is how this might sound:

Earlier, we spoke about how you plan to transition from AWS to Azure. Now that I have had a chance to think about that, I have some new ideas, and I thought it might be a good opportunity to revisit that topic. Since you asked me about my level of exposure to Azure, let me just ask you, what level of experience do you all currently have with Azure? What steps have you implemented to prepare for that transition?

Still another example is where you might say:

Earlier, I asked about how you are planning to migrate from AWS to Azure. I am so thankful for everything you explained on that topic. Can we talk more about that? It was helpful for me to hear about how you plan to make the switch. Now, could I hear more on how you decided to make that switch?

Or:

During the technical interview, I recall asking you all about the choice between two specific paths forward. We had just scratched the surface of what the hypothetical next steps could have been. We ran out of time, so could we revisit that topic now?

Using the opportunity to revisit earlier topics could also sound a bit more like:

I think one of the most interesting questions anyone has asked me was when you asked, "What makes you want to stand on a chair and yell?" I thought it was a quirky question, and I think it was aimed to help me reveal my personality and perhaps a bit of information about topics that I care strongly about. Let me ask you all now, too, what makes you want to stand on a chair and yell?

Another example, while interviewing with the CEO:

Earlier, when I was in the technical interview, I asked the team how amenable they were to the prospect of working with a new data scientist who has thus far worked mostly in R when the team, your team, works mostly in Python. Do you have thoughts or feelings on this topic? What advice, if any, would you have for a new hire coming to your company who has experience with tools and tech stacks not among your company's preferences?

Focus on the Data Culture

My second piece of advice for responding to this important question (What questions do you have for us?) is to focus on the data culture. Data culture is a set of data-related customs, traditions, language, and similar artifacts that members of the company share and pass on from one generation of employees to the next.

Example questions that focus on data culture are:

- *When your team or organization conducts an analysis, have you thought through and documented the steps while you work? And if so, can you walk me through those steps? I would be interested in knowing more about how you divide up the steps of your analytical process or approach.*

217

- *How do you identify and keep track of your research questions / analytical tasks / or business problems that need study or solving? Is there a specific backlog? Do you use a whiteboard? A shared document? Or is it more casual / less formal? Have you adopted the popular Agile framework?*
- *Who has the ability to propose research questions / analytical tasks / or business problems to the team?*
- *How do you prioritize which research questions / analytical tasks / or business problems will be studied sooner rather than later?*

Of course as you adapt these questions for your own voice and personality you might think of them differently. You might even present them differently than I have written above. For example, some speakers might more naturally frame these as statements but while meaning them to be questions. Here are some additional examples.

- *I would be interested in understanding who has the ability to propose research questions / analytical tasks / or business problems to the team.*
- *I would be interested in understanding how you prioritize which research questions / analytical tasks / or business problems will be studied sooner rather than later.*

Chapter Summary

To distil this chapter's advice into one core concept: Frame your approach to the interview process as a discussion. Approaching the experience as a discussion lets you focus on building relationships with your interviewers, which naturally helps to reduce your stress. This stress reduction is especially helpful when you will face challenging questions.

Another tip for reducing interview stress is to be prepared with information regarding the organization. To learn about an organization, I wrote extensively about leveraging their past and present organizational charts.

This chapter also outlined multiple positions you may encounter through the search and selection process. The chapter describes each position in terms of what they do in the selection process, what they know, and how they can help or hinder your placement or career advancement. These positions include internal recruiter, external recruiter, hiring manager, search committee, hiring panel, recruiting coordinator, and compensation team.

In preparing for a specific type of interview, refer to the 12 types of interviews as defined in this chapter: technical, whiteboard, product sense, behavioral, conversational, direct, case study, practical, stress, meals, panel, and group. Pay close attention to the unique tips for each type of interview. Keep in mind how various employers may differ in how they name these interviews. When in doubt on what to expect, just ask for more information.

During the interview, use the STAR method or the XYZ template. Formulate your responses so they showcase these strengths:

- Strong listening skills.
- Problem-solving capabilities.
- A firm understanding of job-related skills.
- Mathematic expertise.
- That you are a rock star communicator and communication facilitator.
- Business acumen.

Being a mid- to late-career professional can give you an advantage in the sense that you already have real-world examples of how you have exemplified these traits in a professional role. Again, do not downplay your previous experiences. These previous experiences could be what sets you apart from the crowd.

You do not need to be an expert in everything.

Ask questions.

CHAPTER 9

Preparing for Negotiations

It is common to experience low or moderate levels of confidence when preparing for and conducting job offer negotiations. This chapter will discuss that lack of confidence. This chapter will also discuss the return on investment for anyone who makes a serious effort to negotiate their salary. To further assist on this topic, I will provide an in-depth discussion of multiple salary research resources, along with a review of their relative strengths and weaknesses.

Simplistic formulae will not work well for most candidates in preparing for salary negotiations. For example, a common bit of advice is to establish your salary demands by taking your current salary and then adding 25%. While your salary plus 25% will be on the low end of what you will ask for, the upper end will be another 25% above that number.

So, for example, if your current salary is $50,000, your low-end expectation would be: $50,000 + $12,500 = $62,500. And then your upper-end expectation would be: $62,500 + $15,625 = $78,125.

The reason formulae such as those above fall short is because they will exacerbate income inequalities. Women and minorities, on average, earn less than white male counterparts.[15] Women and other minorities who base their salary expectations on salary history will consequently on average ask for less than the market should provide. Mid- and late-career professionals who transition into data science from lower-paying professions will likewise risk asking for too little if they follow the overly formulaic advice above.

It is necessary to make sure you pursue opportunities to gather intelligence on what they should pay you based on multiple reputable and reliable sources of information. This chapter will guide you through conducting that research as you prepare for salary negotiations.

A smart candidate will deliberate on all aspects of a job offer, including health insurance, employer contributions to retirement, paid leave (vacation, sick time, time to care for sick family), the opportunity for tuition support, etc.

The problem for candidates who might not consider salary to be the most important factor when evaluating a job offer

---

[15] The empirical evidence on this is extensive. In recent years some of my favorite coverage of this topic is from Sarah Kliff at https://www.vox.com (Kliff, 2017; Kliff, 2018). A recent publication has addressed the many nuances associated with how the income distribution changes across multiple intersectional groups. (Alonso-Villar and del Río, 2022).

is that recruiters may demand to know a salary expectation during the first conversation. Sometimes even before the first conversation. And worse, recruiters will screen candidates based on salary.

Figure 9.1

Speaking about Salary

Imagine this in the life of our new friend Jodi.

The discussion starts on LinkedIn or email:

Recruiter: *Hi Jodi, I'm a recruiter at Titan Tech. We have an opportunity to share. Care to chat?*

Jodi: *Okay, sure. Let us set up a chat.*

Later when the conversation continues on the phone:

Recruiter: *What is it that has you on the job market right now?*

The recruiter has asked a question that implies a premise which the recruiter should know might not be true. The recruiter contacted this candidate. How can the recruiter be sure the candidate is searching?

Jodi: *I am not actively searching. But you indicated you have a great opportunity for me. Can you tell me more about that opportunity? If it turns out that I do not think it is a good fit, I can likely help connect you with others who might be a better fit.*

Recruiter: *So, for the right opportunity, you would be willing to move on from your current work?*

Jodi: *Yes.*

Recruiter: *Let us talk about compensation. What salary target do you have in mind?*

The recruiter has asked about salary expectations before even sharing about the position with the candidate, Jodi. This seemingly backwards approach is not an uncommon occurrence. Avoid misreading apparent reversal as an attempt to trick or disorient you. Assume good intentions on the part of the recruiter but remain firm and focused.

Jodi: *Since you contacted me, and I am not sure what the position's details are, I have not worked out what an appropriate salary would be for this position. Also, salary is not my main motivation. Do you have a budget in mind for this position?*

Recruiter: [Mumbles and stutters a bit, as she does not usually get this question.]

Awkward silence. Jodi patiently waits.

Recruiter: [Tries to avoid giving an answer.] *We have a range, and if you have a target in mind,*

I could speak with the team if it happens to be outside of that range.

Jodi: [Repeats the question.] *Great. What is that range you had in mind?*

Recruiter: [Pauses.] *Umm.* [Sound of paper rustling or computer clicking and typing.] *We were looking at $XXX,XXX on the low end and $YYY,YYY on the upper end.*

Jodi: *Okay, thanks. Sounds like it would be worth our while to continue this conversation. What other questions do you have for me?*

Recruiter: *So, what do you know about Titan Tech?*

In the above conversation, the recruiter asked Jodi about their salary expectation. Jodi did not respond to the question. Instead, Jodi answered the question with a question.

After the recruiter's diligent attempt to get a number from Jodi, they again returned with this primary question. Jodi waited out the ensuing pause. Jodi met the recruiter's second attempt to avoid answering with a non-response. Eventually, the recruiter provided information about salary, first.

Jodi has now learned the hiring range for salary. Jodi has also avoided giving a number so high the recruiter will shortsightedly screen Jodi out of the search. Likewise, Jodi has avoided giving a number that is too low, such that Jodi would risk undercompensation.

Most importantly, Jodi will remain in the search. Jodi and the recruiter can continue the conversation, which is of mutual interest. Continuing this conversation will allow Jodi to gather additional information about the company, its benefits, culture, and other factors. If Jodi later receives an offer, there will be an opportunity to speak about salary, but by then, Jodi will feel well-informed and in a much better position to participate in a meaningful negotiation.

Likewise, the recruiter and the employer will have a deeper understanding and a stronger connection with Jodi. The employer will know Jodi's value (high) and be more amenable to discussing salaries that are commensurate with Jodi's professional value for the employer.

There are other patterns that might have unfolded for Jodi and this recruiter. For example:

Recruiter: *What is your current salary?*

Or:

Recruiter: *What was your salary at your previous position?*

It would be reasonable to respond by saying:

Jodi: *I am so glad you brought up the topic of salary. I would like to note that salary is an important factor, but it is not the most important factor for me. But since you raised the topic, what is the budget you have in mind for this position?*

Another option:

Jodi: *I and a few of my colleagues left our former employer because their salary offerings were not competitive. That previous company was not offering a salary that is commensurate with our level of experience within the industry. As a result, my previous salary would not appropriately inform our discussions on this topic. What is the budget you have in mind for this position?"*

And another option:

Jodi: *I am so glad you brought up the topic of salary. What salaries did you provide for the person who most recently held this position? And what salaries did you provide for the five personnel to hold this position before them?*

Researching Salary

Whether you are seeking a new job, entering the workforce after an absence, or simply want a competitive advantage in negotiating your next raise, one piece of information is critical: What should your salary be?

While job candidates regularly research company history, social media profiles of prospective bosses (or co-workers), plus job qualifications and expectations, salary research remains more of a mystery. For example, how many hours have you spent studying for a technical interview? How many blogs or books have you read about acing technical interviews? How many Udemy courses have you enrolled in? How many hours have you spent on Udacity? Compare for a moment the time you have spent on other job search activity but not on researching salary.

According to the results of a survey I conducted, better than a full third (35%) of job candidates admit to conducting no salary research at all (Nelson, 2022a). One in three job candidates rarely research and compare salaries, and less than 1 in 10 job candidates always research salary comparisons.

Negotiating Salary Is Hard

These findings regarding salary research are as startling as they are shocking. Though it is not necessarily the most important factor, salary plays an important role in any job-related decision (Nelson, 2020c). For many, of course, when evaluating a job offer or deciding to remain with a company, salary is at least as important as job expectations, perks, and office relationships.

Negotiating salary is hard. Everything about this topic is hard. For example, merely knowing where to start a salary negotiation is a major obstacle for many professionals. These difficulties are an important reason why more people are not researching salaries. There is another important reason too.

HOW CONFIDENT ARE YOU ON YOUR ABILITY TO FIND ... USEFUL SALARY COMPARISONS?

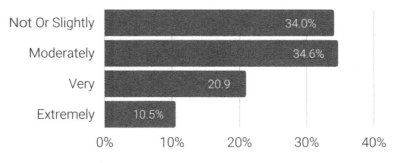

Figure 9.2

A Lack of Confidence

The other reason that leads to insufficient salary research is more fundamental. This fundamental reason relates to another major finding from the above survey: Most people have a lack of confidence when researching salary on their own.

In the same survey mentioned above, over two-thirds of those who responded said they were not, slightly, or only moderately confident in their ability to find useful salary comparisons. A small proportion of respondents, just 10.5%, said they were extremely confident in their ability to find useful data comparisons. Just over 20% said they were very confident.

This lack of confidence is understandable for several reasons, and there are a myriad of factors and dimensions to consider. For example, differences in employment history, skill sets, and geographic location. In many emerging fields, such as data science, educational considerations are difficult to work through because there is no standard career path for the field of data science.

Then there are the roles of bonuses and job perks. And when relying on internet sources, it is difficult to know which sources may be trustworthy. Will you rely on chat rooms, social media, Reddit, Facebook groups, or something else?

This lack of confidence is a problem that outside help, from a professional career coach, can partially solve. Career coaches can help pinpoint salary expectations and help guide you through a successful salary negotiation and other career transitions. As these coaches point out, there is a clear return on investment for those who take the time to conduct salary research. Just what is that return on investment?

The survey referenced above shows:

- Those who conduct salary research are more than 3x more likely to have six-figure incomes.
- Those who use three or more strategies to research salaries may increase their odds of earning a six-figure salary by as much as 15x.

- Of those workers who already have a six-figure income, 90% reported using at least one salary research strategy (Nelson, 2022a).

If only one thing is clear from these statistics, it is this: Those who engage in salary research are in good and high-earning company.

Salary Research Is Not Costly

What is more, salary research is typically low in cost, and it requires only moderate effort and a relatively small amount of time. As you research salaries, keep in mind an important point: A single salary report does not tell the complete story of salaries for your industry. Finding what one other person earns, or what another single organization pays for your role, is not necessarily a definitive indicator of what you should earn. You need more information.

Salary research, as you will see, is a holistic and multipart process. At each part along the way through this process, you will discover many data points. While discovering each data point, each salary you find simply gives a single data point. In the final analysis, combine all the data points before arriving at a well-informed conclusion.

Salary Research Strategies and Resources

Before you go into any salary negotiation, you must objectively determine how much someone in your position should earn. Salaries range widely based on industry, seniority, and geography. Your compensation research should go beyond your take-home pay. It should factor in benefits, such as retirement plan matching, health savings account deposits, transportation, meal allowances, training, and more. It should also include factors related to how in-demand your skill set is—if you find your industry is currently awash with unemployed workers, you may have a harder time negotiating a favorable salary.

Use Your Own Personal Network

Using your own personal network is a useful salary research strategy for those who are in the middle or latter part of their career. Mid- and late-career professionals have likely developed an extensive network of co-workers, former associates, old bosses, favorite instructors, and mentors who are well-entrenched in their industry and have broad visibility and experience with salaries. Now is the time to put that network to work for you.

Your personal network may be comprised of people who are involved in interviewing, making job offers, and ultimately hiring employees with similar skill sets and job descriptions.

Of course, this brand of communication requires discretion. Going in cold and quizzing anyone about their compensation may feel invasive. It is generally taboo to talk about salary and money. The opportunity to discuss the subject of salary may not come about naturally. Below are suggestions on how to break the ice in ways that will not feel invasive.

For example, when you are maintaining or reviving your interpersonal connections, the opportunity to chat about a specific topic (in this case, salary) can help bring a sense of purpose to your discussions. By being clear and upfront with your contacts that you have an interest in chatting about this topic, you will bring a sense of purpose to your networking efforts. Another helpful step is to let your contacts know that you would be happy to share with them the combined results of all your discussions.

If you promise to deliver the results of your conversations, be sure to follow through. This way, when it is time to reconnect again another time, your contacts will remember that you provided them with valuable information through your discussions.

As it turns out, while some may hesitate to share salaries, many others might not.

Once you have established the topic, specific questions that may feel less invasive are:

- *What salary ranges are you seeing?*
- *How are those salaries growing (or not)?*
- *What factors are impacting pay and compensation?*
- *How have you noticed employers tend to respond on counteroffers?*

Call Human Resources

Human resource professionals—recruiters, hiring managers, and others who are in the business of hiring data professionals—typically have a thorough understanding of what the salary landscape looks like.

Those in human resources are broadly familiar with salary expectations, and for good reasons. They often play (or may have previously played) a direct role in making job offers, monitoring merit increases, and assessing pay based on salary audits. These professionals know how salary may be based on feedback from employees, C-suite executives, compensation consultants, legal counsel, and other information sources.

Recruiters, hiring managers, and others who are in the business of hiring professionals can be a valuable source of pay rate intelligence.

Be direct. Simply get a human resource professional on the phone. A logical place to start would be those in your personal network with whom you already have a connection. Look for human resource professionals who can tell you about the salaries they are offering. You can also ask for referrals from your own network. Ask members of your network something like, "Hey, I am doing some salary research, and I want to speak with human resource professionals. Can you help me connect with a trusted human resource professional who might help me out?"

It is also okay to contact recruiters, hiring managers, and human resources professionals that you do not yet already know. Upon reaching these new contacts, see if they will share information about salaries they have recently offered (or advertised). This form of outreach (cold calling) could be the start of building a mutually beneficial and long-term relationship on which you might both rely down the road.

If you use this strategy, prepare to hear a disappointing, "No." If the first contact says no, do not give up. Keep going. With a reasonable amount of effort, this strategy will likely turn up a new contact who will provide useful information.

Contact Recruiters

Another valuable resource is any recruiter who may have contacted you in the past. You may have previously rolled your eyes at one of many well-intentioned recruiters who wrote you via LinkedIn. But these recruiters can be a helpful resource in multiple ways.

Most mid- and late-career professionals in a data-related field have received at least a few contacts from recruiters. Check your email history and your message history on LinkedIn for recruiters who may have reached out to you at any point throughout your career. It may have been years since they contacted you. However, they reached out to you at least once, which means that at one point in your career, they were interested in speaking with you. Their contact with you was likely highly transactional, as they were looking to sell you as a candidate to their client. It is never too late to respond to such recruiters with your own, admittedly transactional, request.

A happy relationship with a well-respected recruiter can be a professional asset. This form of outreach (warm) could also lead to a mutually beneficial and long-term relationship.

The Bureau of Labor Statistics

The U.S. Bureau of Labor Statistics (https://www.bls.gov) is a unit of the United States' Department of Labor and is the primary fact-finding agency for the government in the field of labor statistics. The agency states that it publishes regular updates on the U.S. Consumer Price Index (CPI), the Producer Price Index (PPI), and the U.S. Import/Export Price Indexes (MXP), and provides household data, unemployment statistics, labor productivity, occupational employment projection, layoff statistics, and more.

Of most interest to those conducting salary search are the data related to salaries and salary statistics. According to sites like Investopedia and results from scholarly studies, data from the U.S. Bureau of Labor Statistics are considered highly accurate, objective, relative, and timely.

The BLS provides salary information in many forms. You can find national compensation data, employee benefits, wages by occupation and area, earnings by demographics, and earnings by industry.

A word of warning: While the Bureau of Labor Statistics provides an enormous amount of information regarding pay, the site can be complex and appear hard to use. Therefore, it is useful to look for user guides and YouTube tutorials showing how to extract the information you need from the site. There is also a detailed help and tutorials page (https://www.bls.gov/help).

Salaries Open Data

GovSalaries (https://govsalaries.com) is another extremely comprehensive resource that lets you search by payrolls (including federal, city, county, and state) and by employer, employee, or job title.

The ability to search for salaries of specific people can be especially helpful and revealing. This is a popular site that government employers sometimes use when benchmarking their salaries. As with many of the sites presented throughout this section, keep in mind that as a candidate you may be reviewing salary information on which your prospective employers may also rely as they plan salary and compensation and also plan for salary negotiation. Some users have found that salary information posted about particular individuals is incorrect and cannot be removed, revised, or updated. Another potential drawback is the information may be out of date.

Federal Pay: The Civil Employee's Resource

While these sites (https://www.federalpay.org and http://www.fedsdatacenter.com) call themselves "a free public resource for United States Government employees," there is also much for employees in other sectors.

These sites provide information specific to U.S. federal government employment, and its helpful set of features includes multiple calculators. These sites, however, have a focus on military and law enforcement positions, and they do not appear to have comprehensive salary information for every state. These two sites are also peppered with ads and even some pop-ups.

State-Specific Salary Information Websites

State and federal agencies are valuable sources of income information. Keep in mind that many states and agencies will publish salary information on third-party sites, such as newspapers and industry publications, and many of these resources make the data freely accessible.

Two of the best are Transparent California (https://transparentcalifornia.com) and The Texas Tribune (https://salaries.texastribune.org). Both sites are must-stops in the process of conducting salary research. These sites can be enormously helpful for residents of Texas and California. Both of these state-specific sites present useful, specific and granular information.

These California and Texas sites can also be useful for residents of other states who find it difficult to locate their own state-specific data. Another reason Texas and California are useful is that the populations for these two states are very high. And with many urban or rural locations across the states of California and Texas, you may regard them as representative of many places across the United States.

States themselves and many state government watchdogs make salary data readily available, and in most cases, you can search salaries for specific people. *The Texas Tribune*, for example, maintains an extensive and up-to-date list of state employees—their titles, departments, and salaries—meaning you can search by position, department, or name.

Aggregate sites like https://govsalaries.com publishes similar information, though in many cases, the data are a year or two old. Because the data are sometimes dated, it is important to adjust these numbers based on estimated rates of pay increase.

Other Websites and Data Sets

A variety of websites offer salary and compensation data but aim their services toward employers and recruiters. Some of these sites offer information that may be helpful for candidates. For example, https://openpayrolls.com is a research tool that provides free access to millions of public compensation records in accordance with public record laws. OpenPayrolls focuses on information from employers in the United States and is not specifically associated with, operated by, or endorsed by any government or branch of government. Shortly before this book's publication, OpenPayrolls did not provide salary information for *data scientist*, but provided information for *computational and data science research specialist*.

Another place to look, while keeping in mind the source is intended for employers, is https://www.salary.com, which offers a service called CompAnalyst. This CompAnalyst service seeks to provide employers with the data and insights that may support pay-related decisions. Salary.com advertises itself as a source of solutions addressing the entire compensation process by helping employers quickly price jobs and analyze their compensation and pay practices.

Over at Kaggle, and occasionally from other internet forums, readers can find data related to salary in data science and in other fields. For example, one data set provides information related to individual salaries and reports multiple individual's total gross salary amount paid, the role worked, the employer's main office or contracting branch, and the average number of people who worked for the company (Bhatia, 2022). A search on Reddit's r/datasets also returns data that may be useful for candidates who are interested in looking into salary related data beyond the sources listed above: (https://www.reddit.com/r/datasets).

***

If you want to come to the negotiation table armed with excellent reasons for a pay raise, knowing the full salary landscape for folks with your experience in the roles you seek throughout the industry is key. Understanding how other employers in your field pay for similar work will keep you abreast of industry trends and lead to better decision-making.

Chapter Summary

It is common to lack confidence while negotiating salary. Unfortunately, it is also common to lack confidence in one's ability to find relevant salary comparisons. Yes, salary research is complicated, but when done correctly, it may not require as much effort and time as you think. This chapter discussed a full range of resources available to you that will ease the process of preparing for and then conducting salary negotiations.

As a final thought: Salary is not the only measure of a job's worth. According to my personal tally, as many as half of all workers may consider other factors to be more important than salary. As you review the results of your research, realize that salary alone may not tell the whole story. Some may accept lower pay to live in a more attractive city, or to live closer to family. Others may forgo higher salaries in exchange for access to training and promotion opportunities (or other non-monetary benefits) that are not available elsewhere.

As others may well know, salary at almost any level cannot make up for a dysfunctional workplace, an awful boss, or your unhappiness. Truisms are phases or common understandings that are often, but not always true. They are almost always relatable and then frequently helpful to keep in mind. A truism is worth keeping in mind at this and at all stages of the job search and the transition process: employees do not leave jobs, they leave bosses. Keep these intangible factors in mind as well.

CHAPTER 10

Congrats, You Got the Job!

You received the call; you got the job! #HappyDance Once your celebration is over, you may think, *OK, now what?* I will let you in on a secret: Once you start working, you are going to make mistakes. Just be ready to learn from them and use them to increase your knowledge of the organization and your position.

This chapter will focus on the time period when you start your first role in data science. It will offer advice on how to anticipate the inevitable mistakes, manage those mistakes, continue your conversations from the interviews, and planning your time in the new position. Before concluding this chapter, I will provide guidance on how you can work to share your experiences in ways that may help others.

In Chapter 2, I explained a serious mistake I made in the course of my data science career (Nelson, 2020b). My mistake related to under-communicating how we had been using data science throughout the organization. The extent of my under-communication is that others did not understand how we had been using data science. In fact, they did not realize that we had been using data science at all. Let this chapter help you see that while mistakes are inevitable, you can manage, mitigate, and learn from them.

As a data scientist, I have memorized a handful of models. These models "predict" outcomes many new employees will experience. These outcomes are a function of being in a new role at a new organization. In general, these models are just how the world works. For example, my professional prediction as a data scientist is that you will make many mistakes in your first 90 days. After landing that first (or next) position in data science, nearly everyone makes mistakes.

It gets worse. You will make more mistakes in the next 90 days. Your job is to do three things with those mistakes. First, make sure the number of mistakes you make in any given day decreases when compared to the previous days. If one day goes comparatively worse than its preceding day, do not worry. Think of your goal as beating a moving average. Secondly, anticipate your mistakes and manage any associated harm or risk to minimize the cost of those mistakes. Third, learn from those mistakes.

To visualize these three objectives, imagine charts similar to those shown here. These charts approximate how over time, the number of mistakes (and the cost and harm of those mistakes) should decrease, while the information gained from those mistakes should increase.

The Number Of Mistakes Over Time

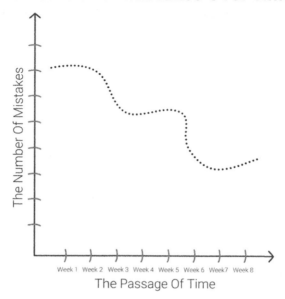

The Cost Of Mistakes Over Time

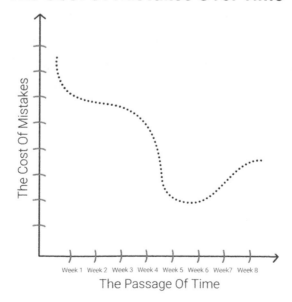

Value Learned From Mistakes Over Time

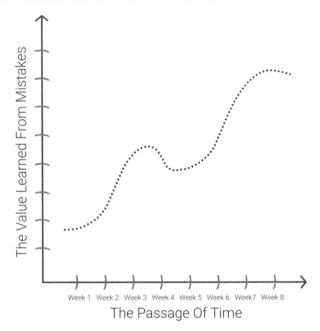

The Passage Of Time

My hope for this chapter is that it will help you avoid some of the mistakes that might be typical for many newer data scientists. For the mistakes this chapter cannot help you avoid, I hope it might help you mitigate the negative consequences of those mistakes. The goal is for you to learn from those mistakes.

How It Feels to Be Highly Experienced but New

Poleh's experience shows how it feels to be highly experienced but newer in a field or a job. Her experiences closely match the experiences of many other mid- or late-career professionals.

Having experienced her earliest years of life without the influence of technology that many younger professionals experienced, Pol does not instinctively feel an urge to rely on technology. Pol knows that technology is a means to an end and not an end in itself. Technology is merely the means to succeed. For example, she was successful in school, even though her earlier schooling did not include in-depth computer or technology education, which many students who were born after her now experience.

Pol worked as a marketing director before finding her way and switching to working as a data scientist. She has maintained her healthy skepticism for technology, even though her data science positions embrace a constantly updating technological landscape. Her marketing background has influenced her opinions toward the value of good communication.

As someone who had to train, later in life, to become proficient with technology, she made many mistakes while navigating the world of technology. She enjoys sharing career mistakes with other professionals to help them understand that it is okay to be imperfect.

If she had allowed those mistakes to discourage her, she may have given up on pursuing data science. She may have missed out on the rewarding career path that she has found in data science. Instead, she learned from her mistakes. As a result of her learning, she was able to reduce the number of mistakes she made over time. Each mistake was a lesson that she made sure not to repeat.

A key lesson that seemed to repeat itself throughout Poleh's career before she transitioned into data science was the importance of communication. As a result of these lessons (mistakes), Pol strongly agrees that better communication helps reduce mistakes. Better communication can reduce the harm that results from a mistake. Also, better communication can improve how individuals and a team learns from mistakes.

Poleh learned, over time, that her natural skepticism toward technology could be an asset for her and her organization. As Pol's job had everything to do with data and technology, her skepticism helped the company avoid hasty approaches as she passed her more critical eye over new ideas and initiatives. Poleh astutely noticed the potential for risks that others may have missed.

It became Poleh's job, in an informal sense, to be her team's sentinel. As a sentinel, she watched the team's course for the future. The niche she filled was that she helped the team identify potential risks. Through intentional conversations designed to build data culture, she also helped the team derive potential solutions or mitigation strategies.

In these ways, Poleh did what many mid- and late-career professionals can do well. She leveraged the skills, abilities, and assets she had acquired by virtue of her experience. She learned from her mistakes and let those lessons provide value for her team and her employer.

Converting mistakes, and experience, into value required meticulous attention to detail, of course. Creating this value required time and energy, too. It was Poleh's willingness to use the skills, abilities, and experiences she had gained as a mid- to late-career professional that let her diminish or mitigate the loss from any one mistake while simultaneously maximizing the value gained.

As a mid- or late-career professional, you can emulate Poleh's experiences as she transitioned her career into data science. The remainder of Chapter 10 focuses on how to position yourself in your new role as a leader who can bring the skills, abilities, and assets you have gained over the course of your career to support the work of your new colleagues, managers, and employers.

Intentional Conversations

Consistent with the advice from earlier chapters that discussed communicating with employers before, during, and after the interview, this chapter's advice continues with the theme that you should ask questions. Ask as many questions as you can. Planning and pursuing intentional conversations are important components of the advice from Poleh's story.

So, you spark intentional conversations by asking questions. Your questions need to be intentional and well-informed, of course. When thought through, asking questions during your early days in a new position will help you perform well in your new role. Asking the right question can be viewed as a team contribution in and of itself.

Below are a set of questions you should ask during your earliest conversations with your new supervisors, stakeholders, and co-workers. It is important to make an effort to ask these kinds of questions as intentionally as possible. For example, say to those who you will work with regularly, "I have a series of questions. When would be a good time to go over them?" Saying you have questions and asking for a good time to go over your questions will make your conversations more intentional.

You might start into your questions and realize you are speaking with the wrong person, or that you need to include others, or the time you selected is not quite right. Keep your mind open to identifying these scenarios, and when you do, consider saving your questions to revisit later.

Here are example questions that focus on learning about the organization's data culture and its data literacy. These questions come from my experience. Mostly, these are questions I had overlooked early on in my career. Many of these questions draw on my experience as a consultant, when I am on a project that aims to help clients build, grow, or enhance their data science culture.

CONGRATS, YOU GOT THE JOB!

The following phrase prefaces each of these questions:

For my team's and my organization's purposes . . .

. . . what is data?

. . . what is a data set?

. . . what is an analysis? What does it mean to conduct an analysis?

. . . when conducting an analysis, what are the expected project inputs and what are the expected project outputs?

. . . what steps do we expect to follow in the course of an analysis or project? Who is involved in which steps?

. . . who in the organization has the authority to commit teams (and other resources) to conducting a specific analysis?

. . . how do we track research questions / analytical questions / business problems we want to study or solve?

. . . how do we prioritize the research questions / analytical questions / business problems we want to study or solve? Who has the authority to decide which we work on now or later?

A Day in the Life

A data scientist's life is all about data. The position title gives away as much. Finding, extracting, manipulating, cleaning, preparing, handling, and analyzing data to leverage it as a valuable resource is a data scientist's reason for being. If data are the new oil, then data science, artificial intelligence, machine learning, and advanced analytics professionals are the new oil refineries.

I usually explain the most common tasks a data scientist will complete daily with reference to Figure 2.1 as shown earlier in Chapter 2, which shows a typical data science process. Of course, the data scientist does not perform every function in every step. The data scientist will contribute to each step. It requires a team to accomplish the entire process. Below is how the data scientist contributes to each step.

Define a Problem

 Early on in a data science project, the data scientist contributes to identifying an analytical question or specifying a business problem to solve. When you can thoroughly define a problem, you are halfway to solving that problem. Oftentimes, organizations or teams will have more questions than they can ever solve. Consequently, the data scientist has a role in both identifying questions or problems and weighing in on which questions may be more readily answerable or which problems may be more readily solvable.

Look and Check Around

Looking and checking around involves researching whether anyone has already asked and answered the question (or solved the problem). If yes, it is also important to find out which data and methods others previously used to answer the question or solve the problem. A daily expectation for data scientists is to be familiar with common data sources and common methods. The data scientist can then expedite the team's process as it looks and checks around. If no one has already asked the question or solved the problem, another important expectation for data scientists is to provide input and insight as to why.

Justification

An important step in the data science process is to justify the work. Before the team reaches the justification stage, some amount of justification has occurred throughout the process of identifying which questions or problems to address. This is especially true when others have previously studied these questions or solved these problems. A data scientist (in collaboration with others) needs to provide input as to why a replication of the work may be worthwhile. Perhaps earlier work required data that was not yet available, but that is now available. Likewise, perhaps the team only now has access to tools or methods that did not yet exist when the earlier work was made.

Gather, Collect, and Wrangle Data

Frequently, but not always, data scientists will have assistance from other specialized data professionals in the gathering, collecting, extracting, and early portions of data preparation. However, data scientists must contribute to data wrangling, too. How data look in production is almost never how data will look when properly prepared for advanced analytics. As crude oil needs to be refined into a usable energy source, similarly, data sets need to be preprocessed. Preprocessing includes finding and handling missing values and broken records, and sometimes augmenting and enhancing the data.

Data scientists will often spend portions of each day working to wrangle data. This work is important because the approach chosen by data scientists may profoundly affect the result and analyses. Making good choices during this step is an essential task in the daily life of a data scientist.

Select and Apply Analytical Techniques

This is the stage when a data scientist will review a range of tools and techniques to find those that are most appropriate for the project at hand. A data scientist may review multiple statistical and mathematical techniques or algorithms in daily practice. This requires research and documentation review, which can be tedious. As each question or problem is unique, this part of a data scientist's daily experience will not go away over time. Following tool and technique selection, the data scientist will then apply those tools and techniques to the data.

Check and Recheck Results

 During this portion of the data science process, a data scientist will perform multiple checks to ensure that the data were sufficient to the project and prepared appropriately, and that they executed the analysis as expected. In the case of developing predictive models, the data scientist will ensure the models generalize well to previously unseen data. The data scientist must work with others to evaluate, identify, and then reduce bias (or otherwise reduce the harmful effects of that bias).

Interpretation and Dissemination

 Data scientists may devote portions of their daily practice to interpreting results. Interpretation involves explaining what the results mean. It also involves identifying, documenting, and then communicating throughout the team any strengths and weaknesses of the work. Following interpretation, the team will need to disseminate the results.

Dissemination, discussed further below, involves communicating the results to those who requisitioned the work—those who asked the questions or who were facing the business problem. These last steps also involve planning for next steps and identifying additional questions that will need further or more careful analysis in future iterations of the process.

Adjacent to the processes (as outlined in Figure 2.1 and as described here) are tasks related to optimization, evaluation, and maintenance. In the case of having solved a business problem, and then having put that solution into production, there is additional ongoing work. Even though the solution may be deployed, data scientists have to continue their evaluation to improve (or maintain) the quality of that solution. Through optimization, the solution is further refined to perform even more effectively over time.

Planning, Tooling, Science, and Dissemination

Because this book is for established professionals, I ask you to think back on the early days of your career, be that 5, 10, 15, or more years ago. As you think about how you spent your time earlier in your career, consider what your main tasks were. You can dissect your work tasks into major categories.

How you spent your time earlier in your career will differ from how you spend your time as a data scientist. This section outlines how you might spend your time in data science by dividing the work into four major categories.

Roughly speaking, it is possible to divide data science into four broad sets of categorical tasks, including planning, tooling, science, and dissemination. A useful way to understand what to expect in your career as a data scientist is to consider how you will spend your time in each of these four categories. Keep in mind that how you will distribute your time across the four categories will evolve.

Figure 10.4 illustrates how you might expect to spend your time in the first few weeks of a new job in data science.

The Work In Your First Few Weeks Of Data Science
As a proportional stacked bar chart - Approximated Values

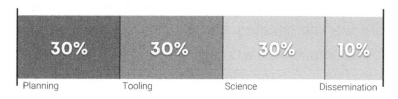

Figure 10.4

Planning

This is the process associated with selecting a question that needs to be answered. Sometimes, *finding a question* is better framed as *selecting a problem that needs to be solved* or *specifying an analytical task*. Planning involves checking whether anyone else has already answered the question you intend to study, or if anyone else has solved the problem you think your work might also solve.

During the planning process, you may find that others have already studied your question or solved your problem of interest. In such situations, you then have the option to review that previous work. You may decide that results from previous work now informs your new work. Despite the valuable information you can gain from previous efforts, there may be unanswered questions which now will need your renewed efforts to fully answer.

Avoid making the mistakes that I described in Chapter 2. The planning work you perform is often not highly visible. To avoid my mistakes, make your planning work more visible. For example, if you are new to an organization, consider offering presentations within the workplace that share an overview of how you will proceed with the planning and development of your work. If situated within a team, make sure you do these presentations as a collaboration. Make the presentation attractive for non-data scientists to attend. Consider calling it "The Top X Data Science Techniques We Plan to Deploy This Coming Fiscal Quarter." X will be the number of techniques you can deploy and discuss.

Another way to make this planning work more visible is to develop a system that will track the research questions and business problems you and your team are considering. A systematic process that tracks and records what questions or problems you are considering, plus which you decide to study now or save for later (and why), will document the valuable work that happens under this planning umbrella.

Tooling

Tooling involves selecting the tools that will be best suited for answering the questions you establish in your planning work. If you specified a business problem to solve, your tool selection process will focus on tools that may help solve that specific problem. This tooling process means reviewing existing tools and methods. Tooling also often means customizing existing tools or building new tools.

Some of the most successful data teams have built their reputation on creating and sharing new tools. A prominent example of a team that has shared its tools is the Urban Institute. They developed a robust set of data retrieval tools, such as the Education Data Explorer (https://educationdata.urban.org/data-explorer), which anyone may now freely use (Chartoff, 2018).

As you look to avoid mistakes related to under-communicating your work, consider replicating the success modeled by the Urban Institute. If you develop new tools, and if you can share them (internally or externally), doing so can be a strategy that will make your work more visible.

Science

Science is the process of asking and answering a question based on empirical observation (data collection and analysis), and then disseminating the results. For the purposes of this chapter, I define *science* as the time and attention given to collecting data and executing the plans laid out earlier. This means applying the previously selected tools and methods to that data. Science also involves tuning models and parameters, plus interpreting, comparing, and otherwise writing about results for the next important set of tasks under dissemination.

Communicating about the science is an arduous task. Keeping your notes and records in place is an effective way to ensure that your scientific work is visible throughout the organization. Having a good set of notes and records will support you as you move into your dissemination work, which is inherently about communicating your results.

Dissemination

Dissemination is the process of reporting results, which can occur in many ways, including internal memos, reports, journal publications, articles, white papers, or discussions. Dissemination may also involve preparing models and other technical specifications for engineers to implement in production as well as making presentations for small or large groups, internally or externally. Dissemination is where you share the original question or problem, reveal your answers or solutions, and describe your data and methods. Another important aspect of dissemination is transparently sharing your work's relative strengths and weaknesses.

Even though dissemination may seem to be the most obvious opportunity to make sure your work is visible, it is not smart to rely entirely on dissemination. As described above, it is important to ensure you communicate your work along the way. Once you begin formally disseminating your results, be sure to emphasize the new questions your results raised. By emphasizing those new questions, you will consequently give added exposure to the planning work.

Allocating Your Time as a Data Scientist

The math on this can be relatively simple. Knowing that you must distribute your time across these four categories of work can help you think about a day, week, month, or fiscal quarter in the life of a data scientist.

I break out the math consistent with the chart shown here, which shows how many data scientists might allocate their time in the first few weeks on a new job. Over a 40-hour work week, 30% of your time equates to about a day and a half, or 12 hours. Over a 20-day month, you will spend about 6 days on planning.

Likewise, you can expect to spend the same amount of time on tooling as well as science. This leaves four hours in the week for dissemination. In a 20-day month, that will be about 2 days of work on dissemination.

Data Science Process	Time Spent/Week	Time Spent/Month
Planning (30%)	12 hours or 1.5 days	6 days
Tooling (30%)	12 hours or 1.5 days	6 days
Science (30%)	12 hours or 1.5 days	6 days
Dissemination (10%)	4 hours or .5 days	2 days

After the first few weeks pass, how you spend your time as a data scientist will shift and change. Starting out, you are not likely to disseminate much because you have not yet had an opportunity to complete an analysis and produce results for dissemination. By your second or third fiscal quarter in your new role as a data scientist, you can expect that your time spent on planning and tooling will diminish while your time spent on science and dissemination will increase.

Data Science Process	Time Spent/Week	Time Spent/Month
Planning (30%)	4 hours or .5 days	2 days
Tooling (30%)	4 hours or .5 days	2 days
Science (30%)	20 hours or 2.5 days	10 days
Dissemination (10%)	12 hours or 1.5 days	6 days

As shown by these figures, the amount of actual science performed tends to be limited toward the beginning of the cycle, and it may not reach 50% science until well into the second year. Eventually, the time spent on science will increase. Then, the time spent on science may continue to fluctuate. The reason the time spent on science may fluctuate over time is because following that increase in scientific work, the work will then immediately shift to dissemination. Dissemination is important because that is when you share your work with others, get feedback on your work, and then use that feedback on the next iteration or project.

Continuing to look further ahead, late in the second or third year, there will likely be less focus on tooling because the tooling work executed early in the first or second years should be reusable. The time you spent on tooling early in the first year you can now spend on other tasks, including planning, science, and dissemination. Following the initial 2 years, a routine will develop.

Paying Your Success Forward

At the end of Chapter 4, I shared a story about balloons piled in a hallway. It is a fun story about how finding success is a massive challenge when attempted on your own. However, finding success with the help of others moves things along more quickly and smoothly.

It is important to help others. When you have experienced success through hard work, dedication, and savvy strategy, it is wise to share your thoughts, ideas, and experiences so that others can learn from you.

Everyone has a meaningful story as the result of their experiences. Mid- and late-career professionals have stories that may be valuable for others to hear. Each one of us has something to share with another person trying to achieve success in their life. Once you transition into data science, you have even more value to offer by sharing your story.

I am asking readers to pay their success forward. One of the easiest and most helpful ways to pay your success forward is to share your story.

You can answer the call I am issuing here in a number of ways. Start by writing about your experiences in a simple social media post. Make a list of things you know now, after the transition, that you wish you might have known sooner. Another option is to track and make a list of the interview questions you experienced and how you answered them, and then give advice to others on how they might respond. Another simple and pragmatic approach would be to share where you found the job description for the position you now have. Of course, if your new organization is still hiring, make sure you mention that and direct readers to the job board.

If you want to go beyond social media posts, you could record a video or write an article. If you feel comfortable doing so, consider posting on multiple social media platforms. To the extent you are able and willing, consider overtly offering to help others if they reach out to you.

Be authentic and genuine in your approach. When coming from a place of authenticity, others will value and appreciate your help. As a bonus, offering to help others may lead you to form connections that are meaningful and mutually beneficial.

Chapter Summary

Once again, congratulations! You have accomplished your goal of working as a data scientist.

My number one piece of advice at this stage of your journey is to learn to ask well-informed questions frequently. Not only will this practice decrease the number of mistakes you make, but you will also demonstrate your dedication and willingness to learn.

If you need help with the wording, use the sample questions in the "Intentional Conversations" sections of this chapter to get you started. Or imagine what Daveed, Poleh, or Jodi would ask.

If this is your first data science position, or if it is your second or even your fifth, you might be wondering what your workflow should look like. This chapter further discussed the data science process that I previously shared in Chapter 2. This data science process serves as an outline for a data scientist's daily experiences.

Note that this is a rough outline. Your experiences may resemble those described in this chapter, but your experiences will still undoubtably differ, too. You may need to remove, add, or otherwise rearrange these steps to complete your work.

Another approach to thinking about your work is to organize it into four sets of work: planning, tooling, science, and dissemination. The time spent working on each set will ebb and flow depending on where you are in your data science career. However, when you are first starting off, you might expect to spend 30% of your time planning (6 days monthly), 30% tooling (6 days monthly), 30% on science (6 days monthly), and 10% disseminating (3 days monthly). This breakdown is merely an educated guess as to what you might expect.

Through the planning, tooling, science, and dissemination discussion, this chapter is a source of advice that provides specific strategies you can use to make sure your work is visible to others.

Lastly, I closed this chapter with a friendly suggestion to pay your success forward. Others have helped you get to where you are now. Consider how you may advise and inspire those who are at an earlier stage of the same journey.

Retrospective and a Call to Action

After this retrospective, I issue readers a call to action. If you do nothing else after picking up this book, consider answering my call to action. If you do, be sure to tag me on social media (@adamrossnelson)!

One of the most common questions I get is "Why did you become a data scientist?" I am used to this kind of question because before I was a data scientist, I often got "Why did you study law but then work in education?" Put differently, the question was sometimes "Why didn't you practice law?" Another question is, "Why didn't you stay with teaching English?"

How I understood my motivations changed over time. Consequently, my answers to these questions have changed over time. Mid- or late-career professionals may change their career trajectory for multiple reasons. Throughout this book, I acquainted readers with Daveed, Poleh, and Jodi, who, like myself, became data scientists later in their careers.

Of course, Daveed, Poleh, and Jodi are fictional, but I conjured them to help myself and other mid- or late-career professionals think about both transitioning into data science and being a data scientist. My responses to the questions "Why this career option?" or "Why that career choice?" are similar to the responses I imagine Daveed, Poleh, and Jodi would offer.

In Daveed's case, zis career evolved in ways that served Daveed's employer's needs but that did not serve Daveed's interests. For Poleh and Jodi, they both were working as data scientists but not officially. Therefore, transitioning into data science meant earning added compensation and other meaningful experiences that came with a data science career.

When I started writing this book, I sought to offer advice for mid- and late-career professionals looking to transition into data science. In researching, planning, and thinking through my own experiences, plus closely acquainting myself with the experiences of others, I discovered a lack of advice specific to mid- and late-career professionals. There is plenty of advice on transitioning into data science because the field is growing fast, and it is lucrative. Data science has been called *sexy*—as if any career can be that.

In my view, mid- and late-career professionals have a more measured view of career options: We do not choose careers for their sex appeal. We are not looking for *sexy* careers. And even though the financial rewards associated with a career in data science can be substantial, as mid- or late-career professionals, we are usually motivated by other factors beyond a fat paycheck.

In order to help mid- and late-career professionals satisfy their diverse motivations for a career change (into data science), I wrote this book to provide advice and guidance that mid- and late-career professionals will not find any other place. Please consider my call to action.

A Call to Action for You

One of this book's key pieces of advice is to build and leverage your social media presence. In my experience, many are skeptical about a personal social media strategy. I have worked with many personal-branding skeptics.

Forget the label of *personal branding* for a moment. Consider the value of having a ready-to-go online resource of folks who have benefited from knowing you. Because they may have benefited from knowing you, they may be in a position to further assist you in your career. Having that kind of resource in your life is valuable.

Thus, this bit of advice also makes for a quick win that just about anyone reading this book can implement. Here is how:

1. If you are currently employed, find your company's job board.
    a. If you are not currently employed, find the job board of a company where you previously worked.
    b. If you have not previously worked for another company, find a company where someone in your family works.

    c. The main thing is to find a job board, at a company with which you have a personal connection.

2. Find a job that you think would be interesting to your existing social media connections.

    a. If you do not have social media yet, you can follow the advice in Chapter 5 to set up your LinkedIn account.

    b. The main thing is to start some place. You know your existing connections and their interests—even if you have not interacted with them recently.

3. Ask the hiring manager if they would mind if you posted the position on your social media. Be open, transparent, and honest with the hiring manager. Say you want to be more active online and that you read in a book that sharing jobs is a good way to do that. Ask if you can tag that hiring manager.

4. Make a social media post about the job you found.

    a. Summarize the job posting.

    b. Say something about the job or the company that you know (or can infer based on your experience with the company) but that is not in the position description.

    c. Tag the hiring manager if you have permission to do so.

    d. Tag me (@adamrossnelson) if you would like my help amplifying the post.

e. Offer to speak with anyone who might have an interest in the job (or a similar job). Offer to be a resource.

If or when anyone reaches out to you, keep your promise to be helpful. Be willing to answer questions. However, if you do not feel you know the answers, be honest about that and offer to try and find the answer.

When you find the answer, pass it along. On the chance you do not find the answer, circle back to apologize and point your connection toward one or more other resources (if you can find them) that might be helpful.

Finding any job is really about winning a benefit for yourself. Maybe earning is a better word than winning. Whatever the best word is, one of the surest ways to win or earn a benefit for yourself is to provide value and benefits to others.

Works Cited

Alonso-Villar, Olga, & Coral del Río. 2022. "Privilege and Hindrance on the USA Earnings Distribution by Gender and Race/Ethnicity: An Intersectional Framework with 12 groups. *International Journal of Manpower.* https://www.emerald.com/insight/content/doi/10.1108/IJM-12-2021-0705

America Counts Staff. February 21, 2019. "Number of Master and Doctoral Degrees Doubles Among Population." United States Census Bureau. www.census.gov/newsroom/press-releases/2019/education-degrees-double.html

American Community Survey. 2021. "Educational Attainment" (table). United States Census Bureau. https://data.census.gov/table?q=United+States&g=0100000US&tid=ACSST1Y2021.S1501

Bhatia, Ruchi. 2022. "Data Science Job Salaries." Kaggle. Updated June 2022. www.kaggle.com/datasets/ruchi798/data-science-job-salaries

Bowne-Anderson, Hugo. August 15, 2018. "What Data Scientists Really Do, According to 35 Data Scientists." *Harvard Business Review.* https://hbr.org/2018/08/what-data-scientists-really-do-according-to-35-data-scientists

Chartoff, Ben. 2018. "Why We Built an API for Urban's Education Data Portal." Medium. October 16, 2018. https://medium.com/@urban-institute/why-we-built-an-api-for-urbans-education-data-portal-1dc83468e7b

Clance, Pauline Rose. *The Impostor Phenomenon: When Success Makes You Feel Like a Fake.* 1986. New York: Bantam Books. pages 20–22 ("Clance IP Scale") online at: https://paulineroseclance.com/pdf/IPTestandscoring.pdf

Doubek, James. "Attention, Students: Put Your Laptops Away." April 17, 2016. NPR. www.npr.org/2016/04/17/474525392/attention-students-put-your-laptops-away

Eremenko, Kirill. 2018. "The Data Science Process." In *Confident Data Skills: Master the Fundamentals of Working with Data and Supercharge Your Career*, 70–71. London, England: Kogan Page.

European Leadership University. "Data Science Salary in Europe & Best Cities to Work In." June 21, 2019. European Leadership University. https://elu.nl/data-science-salary-in-europe-best-cities-to-work-in/

GitHub Docs. 2022. "Changing Your GitHub Username." GitHub. Accessed October 12, 2022. https://docs.github.com/en/account-and-profile/setting-up-and-managing-your-personal-account-on-github/managing-personal-account-settings/changing-your-github-username

Gizmodo Staff. "Degrees of the Future 2022: Data Science." August 11, 2022. *Gizmodo*. https://gizmodo.com/data-science-college-university-program-degree-1849354958

Glassdoor. "50 Best Jobs in America for 2022." 2022. *Glassdoor*. www.glassdoor.com/List/Best-Jobs-in-America-LST_KQ0,20.htm

Government of Canada Job Bank. "Data Scientist in Canada." last modified November 6, 2022. Government of Canada Job Bank. www.jobbank.gc.ca/marketreport/outlook-occupation/227147/ca

Griset, Rich. "What Does the Future Hold for Master's Degree Programs in Data Science?" March 7, 2022. *Fortune*. https://fortune.com/education/business/articles/2022/03/07/what-does-the-future-hold-for-masters-degree-programs-in-data-science/

Gupta, Nikita. "Master's in Data Science in Canada: Top Universities, Admissions, Cost, Scholarships, Jobs." updated October 28, 2022. Collegedunia. https://collegedunia.com/canada/article/masters-in-data-science-in-canada-top-universities-tuition-and-cost-of-study-admission-process-scholarships-and-job-prospects

Hooper, Rowan. October 13, 2012. "Ada Lovelace: My brain is more than merely mortal." *New Scientist*, 216 (2886): 29. https://doi.org/10.1016/s0262-4079(12)62633-5

IEEE-USA. "IEEE-USA Salary & Benefits Survey Report - 2021 Edition." 2021. IEEE-USA. https://ieeeusa.org/product/ieee-usa-salary-benefits-survey-report-2021-edition/

Jae, H. "The Effectiveness of Closed Caption Videos in Classrooms: Objective versus Subjective Assessments." 2019. *Journal of Instructional Pedagogies*, 22.

Kliff, Sarah. September 8, 2017. "The Truth About the Gender Wage Gap." Vox.com. https://www.vox.com/2017/9/8/16268362/gender-wage-gap-explained

Kliff, Sarah, February 19, 2018. "A stunning chart shows the true cause of the gender wage gap." Vox.com. https://www.vox.com/2018/2/19/17018380/gender-wage-gap-childcare-penalty

Microsoft. "The Styles advantage in Word." Accessed November 23, 2022. Microsoft Support. https://support.microsoft.com/en-us/topic/the-styles-advantage-in-word-b4a6372f-188c-93cb-831b-c4dd0cb3a881

Nantasenamat, Chanin. July 27, 2020. "The Data Science Process." *Towards Data Science*. https://towardsdatascience.com/the-data-science-process-a19eb7ebc41b

Nelson, Adam Ross. 2020a. "Merging Data: The Pandas Missing Output." *Towards Data Science*. January 18, 2020. https://towardsdatascience.com/merging-data-the-pandas-missing-output-dafca42c9fe

———. 2020b. "My Biggest Career Mistake, in Data Science." *Towards Data Science*. April 18, 2020. https://towardsdatascience.com/my-biggest-career-mistake-in-data-science-b95ad9fd0ff7

———. 2020c. "A Quick Poll of Data Science & Research Oriented Professionals, Methods & Results." *Towards Data Science*. November 6, 2020. https://towardsdatascience.com/a-quick-poll-of-data-science-research-oriented-professionals-fd2fd0629d7

———. 2020d. "Reordering Pandas Dataframe Columns: Thumbs Down On Standard Solutions." *Towards Data Science*. February 16, 2020. https://towardsdatascience.com/reordering-pandas-dataframe-columns-thumbs-down-on-standard-solutions-1ff0bc2941d5

———. 2020e. "How To Ask For Help." *Towards Data Science*. April 18, 20202. https://towardsdatascience.com/how-to-ask-for-help-5c24b70c9314

———. 2021. "Beginner Friendly Data Science Projects Accepting Contributions." *Towards Data Science*. January 17, 2021. https://towardsdatascience.com/beginner-friendly-data-science-projects-accepting-contributions-3b8e26f7e88e

———. 2022a. "4 Ways to Revolutionize Your Salary Research." Medium. February 22, 2022. https://adamrossnelson.medium.com/4-ways-to-revolutionize-your-salary-research-f91163e9f995

———. 2022b. "93 Datasets That Load With a Single Line of Code." *Towards Data Science*. May 9, 2022. https://towardsdatascience.com/93-datasets-that-load-with-a-single-line-of-code-7b5ffe62b655

———. 2022c. "A Deep Dive on Domain Knowledge Data Science." *Towards Data Science*. October 12, 2022. https://pub.towardsai.net/a-deep-dive-on-domain-knowledge-data-science-683e871d8206

———. 2022d. "Data Science Projects Accepting Community Contributions." *Towards Data Science*. May 11, 2022. https://towardsdatascience.com/data-science-projects-accepting-community-contributions-662e724ba110

———. 2022e. "Getting to Know Yourself + Preparing for a Successful Job Interview." *Adam Ross Nelson* (blog). November 11, 2022. https://coaching.adamrossnelson.com/blog/first-questions-telling-us-about-yourself.

Occupational Outlook Handbook. last modified September 8, 2022. "Computer and Information Research Scientists." https://www.bls.gov/ooh/computer-and-information-technology/computer-and-information-research-scientists.htm

Palachy, Shay. January 3, 2019. "Data Science Project Flow for Startups." *Towards Data Science.* https://towardsdatascience.com/data-science-project-flow-for-startups-282a93d4508d

The Chronicle of Higher Education. August 19, 2022. https://drive.google.com/file/d/1lVQ322f1eRkC8pjvTczWCeMbrVxnfU8e/view?usp=share_link

WORKS CITED

The Royal Society. "Dynamics of data science skills" (30). May 2019. www.burning-glass.com/wp-content/uploads/dynamics-of-data-science-skills-report.pdf

Sakulku, James and James Alexander. 2011. "The Imposter Phenomenon." *International Journal of Behavioral Science*, 6(1): 73–92.

Scikit-learn. "Contributing." Scikit-learn. https://scikit-learn.org/dev/developers/contributing.html

Statista. "Volume of data/information created, captured, copied, and consumed worldwide from 2010 to 2020, with forecasts from 2021 to 2025 (in zettabytes)." Accessed October 11, 2022. *Statista*. www.statista.com/statistics/871513/worldwide-data-created/

Tukey, J. W. 1962. "The Future of Data Analysis." *The Annals of Mathematical Statistics*, 33(1): 1–67.

U.S. Bureau of Labor Statistics. 2022a. "7.8 million workers had an illness-related work absence in January 2022." *The Economics Daily*. February 9, 2022. https://www.bls.gov/opub/ted/2022/7-8-million-workers-had-an-illness-related-work-absence-in-january-2022.htm

U.S. Bureau of Labor Statistics. 2022b. "Employed Persons by Detailed Occupation and Age." last modified January 20, 2022. https://www.bls.gov/cps/cpsaat11b.htm

Vuleta, Branka. October 28, 2021. "How Much Data Is Created Every Day? +27 Staggering Stats." *SeedScientific*. https://seedscientific.com/how-much-data-is-created-every-day/

Wikipedia contributors. 2022a. "Ada Lovelace." Wikipedia, The Free Encyclopedia. last edited November 15, 2022. https://en.wikipedia.org/wiki/Ada_Lovelace

Wikipedia contributors. 2022b. "Corner Case." Wikipedia, The Free Encyclopedia. last edited January 26, 2022. https://en.wikipedia.org/wiki/Corner_case

Wikipedia contributors. 2022c. "Edge Case." Wikipedia, The Free Encyclopedia. last edited October 10, 2022. https://en.wikipedia.org/wiki/Edge_case

Wikipedia contributors. 2022d. "Peter Naur." Wikipedia, The Free Encyclopedia. last edited November 8, 2022. https://en.wikipedia.org/wiki/Peter_Naur

Wikipedia contributors. 2022e. "Rosetta Stone" Wikipedia, The Free Encyclopedia. last edited October 1, 2022. https://en.wikipedia.org/wiki/Rosetta_Stone

Resources

Educational

365 Data. https://365datascience.com

Analytics Vidhya. https://datahack.analyticsvidhya.com

Data Camp. https://datahack.analyticsvidhya.com

DataLemur. https://datahack.analyticsvidhya.com (referral link: https://datalemur.com/?referralCode=SvPqz919)

Skillsoft. https://www.skillsoft.com

Distributed Portfolio

Carrd. https://carrd.co (referral link: https://try.carrd.co/arn2020)

Driven Data. https://www.drivendata.org/

GitHub. https://github.com

GitHub Archive Program. https://archiveprogram.github.com

Kaggle. https://www.kaggle.com

Maven. https://www.mavenanalytics.io

Medium. https://medium.com (referral link: https://adamrossnelson.medium.com/membership)

Omdena. http://www.omdena.com

Quora. www.quora.com

LinkedIn + Social Media Resources

Canva. https://www.canva.com

Fiverr. https://www.fiverr.com (referral link: http://www.fiverr.com/s2/cf49cb67a5)

Photofeeler. https://www.photofeeler.com

Unsplash. https://unsplash.com

Upwork. https://www.upwork.com

Preparing for Interviews

Daily Coding Problem. https://www.dailycodingproblem.com

Interview Cake. https://www.interviewcake.com

LeetCode. https://leetcode.com

Mimo. https://mimo.org

The Org. http://theorg.com

Select Star SQL. https://selectstarsql.com

SQL Murder Mystery. https://selectstarsql.com

Salary Research

Federal Pay. https://www.federalpay.org and https://www.fedsdatacenter.com

OpenPayrolls. https://openpayrolls.com

Salaries Open Data. https://govsalaries.com

https://www.salary.com

The Texas Tribune. https://salaries.texastribune.org

Transparent California. https://transparentcalifornia.com

The U.S. Bureau of Labor Statistics. https://www.bls.gov

Sentiment Analysis Tutorials

AWS (using Amazon Comprehend): https://aws.amazon.com/getting-started/hands-on/analyze-sentiment-comprehend

Azure (using Azure Synapse): https://learn.microsoft.com/en-us/azure/synapse-analytics/machine-learning/tutorial-cognitive-services-sentiment

Google (using Google Cloud Natural Language API): https://cloud.google.com/natural-language/docs/sentiment-tutorial

Writing

Grammarly. https://www.grammarly.com

Hemingway Editor. https://hemingwayapp.com

ProWritingAid. https://prowritingaid.com (referral link: https://prowritingaid.com/?afid=27636)

Datasets (for training, testing, demonstration, + educational purposes)

93 Datasets That Load With A Single Line of Code. https://towardsdatascience.com/93-datasets-that-load-with-a-single-line-of-code-7b5ffe62b655

https://analytics.usa.gov/data

Data USA. https://datausa.io

European Commission. https://data.europa.eu/en

Five Thirty Eight (News Site). https://data.fivethirtyeight.com

https://www.foreignassistance.gov

Google Dataset Search. https://datasetsearch.research.google.com

LinkedIn: The Best Example Data Source You Never Knew. https://towardsdatascience.com/linkedin-the-best-example-data-source-you-never-knew-737d624f24b7

Open Data Stack Exchange. https://opendata.stackexchange.com

Reddit's r/datasets. https://www.reddit.com/r/datasets

Seaborn. https://seaborn.pydata.org/generated/seaborn.load_dataset.html

Stata Example Data. https://www.stata.com/links/examples-and-datasets

Tableau. https://public.tableau.com/app/resources/sample-data

UC Irvine Machine Learning Repository. https://archive-beta.ics.uci.edu

U.S. Census. https://data.census.gov

U.S. Department of Education's Integrated Postsecondary Education Data System (IPEDS). https://nces.ed.gov/ipeds/use-the-data

Urban Institute's Education Data Explorer. https://educationdata.urban.org/data-explorer

Urban Institute's Urban Data Catalog. https://datacatalog.urban.org/search/type/dataset

Cover Illustration

```python
# Import necessary libraries
import pandas as pd
import numpy as np
from scipy.spatial import distance
import matplotlib.pyplot as plt
import seaborn as sns

# Set Seaborn contexts and styles
sns.set_context('talk')
sns.set_style('white')

# Specify Theta (controls number of shapes)
theta = np.arange(0, 8*np.pi, .3)

# Display for reference the number of shapes
print(f'Making two spirals, each with {len(theta)} shapes.')

# Calculate x and y coordinates
# First Spiral (set a = 1 and b = .05)
x = 1 * np.cos(theta) * np.exp(.05 * theta)
y = 1 * np.sin(theta) * np.exp(.05 * theta)

# Calculate m and n coordinates
# Second Spiral (set a = -1 and b to .05)
m = -1 * np.cos(theta) * np.exp(.05 * theta)
n = -1 * np.sin(theta) * np.exp(.05 * theta)

# Make DataFrame; Put x, y, m, n coordinates in dictionary
data = {'xvar':list(x) + list(m),
        'yvar':list(y) + list(n)}

# Create a Pandas DataFrame from the dictionary
df = pd.DataFrame(data)

# Calculate Euclidean distance between points and center
# Scale by raising to power of 4
dist = []
for row in range(len(df)):
    dist.append(
        distance.euclidean(
            [df['xvar'].iloc[row],
             df['yvar'].iloc[row]],
            [0,0]))

# Add distances for size argument
df['distance'] = np.array(dist) ** 4
```

HOW TO BECOME A DATA SCIENTIST

```python
# Plot figure with point size a function of distance
plt.figure(figsize = (15, 15))
# Turn display of axes off
plt.axis('off')

cover = sns.scatterplot(
    data=df, x='xvar', y='yvar',
    size='distance', sizes=(500, 3000),
    legend=False, marker='h')

# Save the plot as a PNG and SVG file with default color
plt.savefig('cover_art_default_color.png',
            transparent=True, format='png')
plt.savefig('cover_art_default_color.svg',
            transparent=True, format='svg')

# Create two versions plot, (white points + black points)
for i in ['white', 'black']:
    cover = sns.scatterplot(
        data=df, x='xvar', y='yvar',
        size='distance', sizes=(500, 3000),
        legend=False, marker='h', color=i)
    plt.savefig('cover_art_{}_color.png'.format(i),
                transparent=True, format='png')
    plt.savefig('cover_art_{}_color.svg'.format(i),
                transparent=True, format='svg')

# Display the final version of the scatterplot
cover
```

About the Author

Dr. Adam Ross Nelson, JD, PhD, is a career coach and data science consultant. As a career coach, he helps others enter and level up in data-related professions. As a data science consultant, he provides research, data science, machine learning, and data governance services. He holds a PhD from The University of Wisconsin–Madison in Educational Leadership and Policy Analysis. Adam is also formerly an attorney with a history of working in higher education, teaching all ages and working as an educational administrator.

Adam sees it as important for him to focus time, energy, and attention on projects that may promote access, equity, and integrity in the field of data science. This commitment means he strives to find ways for his work to challenge system oppression, injustice, and inequity. He is passionate about connecting with other data professionals in person and online. If you are looking to enter or level up in data science, one of the best places to start is to visit https://coaching.adamrossnelson.com

Connect with Adam Ross Nelson

Coaching website: https://coaching.adamrossnelson.com

Book Bonuses: https://coaching.adamrossnelson.com/book_bonuses

LinkedIn (Adam Ross Nelson): https://www.linkedin.com/in/arnelson

LinkedIn (Up Level Data, LLC): https://www.linkedin.com/company/data-science-career-services

Facebook: https://www.facebook.com/adamrossnelson

Twitter: https://twitter.com/adamrossnelson

Medium: https://adamrossnelson.medium.com